A BALANCED
CHRISTIAN DISCERNS
EXTREMES

Ralph   Woodrow

International Standard Book Number: 0-916938-20-4

A catalog of books and / or information
can be otained by contacting:

RALPH WOODROW
**P.O. Box 21,
Palm Springs, CA 92263-0021**

**Toll-free Order / Message Line: (877) 664-1549
Fax: (760) 323-3982
Email: ralphwoodrow@earthlink.net
Website: www.ralphwoodrow.org**

**Cover design: Miller Studio, Wilmington, DE
www.millerstudio.com**

A BALANCED
CHRISTIAN DISCERNS
EXTREMES

A book about a balanced Christian life, at first glance, may seem less exciting than one with prophetic speculation, or a flamboyant exposé regarding doctrinal differences. But in the long run, the *practical* lessons about balance can be of greater importance.

Anyone who is deeply involved in any profession will learn things about that profession that are not well known. This is true whether he is a politician, lawyer, trash collector, butcher, baker, candlestick maker—or preacher. Over the years, from my youth, I have had the opportunity to travel and speak in hundreds of different churches. In the process, by God's grace, I have learned many lessons about the wisdom of balance.

First, notice our title is an A-B-C-D-E acrostic:

> **A**
> **B** alanced
> **C** hristian
> **D** iscerns
> **E** xtremes

The words that make up this title are solidly rooted in Scripture. Righteous leaders prayed for wisdom to *"discern* between good and bad" (1 Kings 3:9; cf. Heb. 5:14). A wise man *"discerns* both time and judgment"; while others fail to *"discern* between their right hand and their left" (Ecc. 8:5; Jonah 4:11). Spiritual things must be "spiritually *discerned"* (1 Cor. 2:14). *"Discerning* of spirits" is a

1

spiritual gift (1 Cor. 12:10). God's word is "a *discerner* of the thoughts and intents of the heart" (Heb. 4:12).

The *balance*—in use from ancient times—is mentioned several times in Scripture. "A false balance is abomination to the Lord: but a just weight is his delight" (Prov. 11:1, Lev. 19:36, etc.). "You are weighed in the balances, and are found lacking," was a message of doom for Belshazzar (Dan. 5:27). His evil had outweighed the good.

The principle of balance may be seen in the word "moderation," defined as: "avoiding *extremes* of behavior or expression; the observing of reasonable limits." The Bible says: "Let your *moderation* be known to all men" (Phil. 4:5).

Another passage says: "Do not be overrighteous, neither be overwise....It is good to grab the one and not let go of the other. The man who fears God will avoid all *extremes*" (Ecc. 7:16-18, NIV).

"Have you found honey?" asks Proverbs 25:16. "Eat so much *as is sufficient for you*, lest you be filled therewith, and vomit it." This statement—obviously not against honey itself—illustrates how something can be *overdone.*

And, there are the words of Jesus himself—the classic quote about *extremes*—how some "strain out a gnat, and swallow a camel" (Matt. 23:24).

The wisdom of *balance* may also be seen in many practical, commonsense examples:

A person walking a tightrope must not lean too far one way or the other. Even riding a bicycle requires a proper balance.

Equilibrium, a sense of balance, allows one to stand without falling over (cf. 1 Cor. 10:12).

If a string on a musical instrument is twisted too tight, it will not be the proper pitch and may even break! If a string is too loose, it will be out of tune.

Clothes that are too loose or baggy may be impractical; clothes that are too tight may be inappropriate or uncomfortable. As with air temperature, there is a comfort zone, between the extremes.

Trains are balanced on two rails. "Standard gauge" is 4 feet 8½ inches, a measurement based, it is said, on the distance between the wheels of ancient Roman chariots. If the rails vary more than a few inches from the standard, the train will derail. There must be the proper alignment, the correct gauge.

An experienced navigator knows how to properly steer his ship, so that it does not veer off course because of wind or waves. As we become balanced Christians, we learn not to be "tossed to and fro, and carried about with every wind of doctrine" (Eph. 4:14).

A person learning to drive may steer the car too far to the left, and then react by swerving to the right, then back to the left!—causing the car to zigzag down the road. Proverbs 4:27 says, "Turn not to the right hand nor to the left."

The motor in a car must have the correct ratio of air and gasoline—too much or too little will cause it to lose power. If a tire is out of balance, a car will bump and bounce down the road.

If a checkbook is not properly balanced, checks begin to bounce, resulting in bank charges, extra work, frustration, and embarrassment. If a person's life is out of balance, spiritually or otherwise, it can also bring loss and confusion.

GONE TO THE COUNTRY!

Louis Marshall Jones (1913 - 1998), better known to millions of people as "Grandpa Jones," will long be remembered for his banjo picking, singing, and countrified humor. I once heard him tell a story about going to see his uncle who lived in a very remote area. After driving by car as far as he could on the road, he unloaded his bicycle and rode on a trail. At the end of the trail, he continued walking, swinging on vines across chasms and working his way through a dense forest. After many hours, when he finally got to his uncle's house, he was not home. A note on the door explained: "Gone to the country"!

Living far away from civilization, in a hermit existence, is obviously not for everyone! At the other extreme, however—living in an overcrowded, congested, pollution-laden city—is far from ideal. Most people prefer the balance of living somewhere between the two extremes.

A house that is too small crowds everyone together, there is not enough space to put things, and may produce a claustrophobic feeling. On the other hand, as nice as it would be to have a large house, even this could be extreme. If it is too big, it could be more like living in a hotel, with so many rooms. If a kitchen is too large, it becomes impractical, requiring more steps to accomplish the various functions. Ideally, there is a practical norm, a balance, somewhere between the extreme of too small or too big.

One person may buy a large and expensive home far beyond his means, but then fail to enjoy it because of the constant struggle to make the payments. It could be self-defeating. Someone else may buy a cheap house, but if it is in a bad location, or has other problems, considering resale value, it may cost more in the long run.

Some folks spend all the money they get, never saving anything. Others, always trying to save their money, fail to invest. Both are extremes. I knew a man who would drive around a block several times in order to find a parking meter with time on it. While saving a dime, he may have spent three times as much in effort and gasoline!

Have you ever heard of buying postage stamps for *less* than their face value? I had not, either; but back in the 1960s, a stamp dealer in Arizona said he could mail us

$100 worth of stamps for $80. Sure enough, I received the stamps for this price. They were all valid stamps, but they were old—leftovers, I assume. Some were holiday stamps from years past. They were all odd amounts—13 cents, 7 cents, 3 cents, some (if I recall correctly) were even amounts like 1½ cents!

It ended up, packages of books we mailed were decorated with an interesting variety of stamps! Postal clerks were amused—many of the stamps they could not remember seeing before. Though these stamps cost less money, it took five times as long to use them. The time involved offset any benefit. Sometimes the *cheap* way of doing things costs *more!*

A businessman must find a balance between charging too much, or too little, for his product. If he does not charge enough, he will not stay in business; if he charges too much, customers will go elsewhere.

If one pays a small price for a meal at a restaurant, and the food is not very good, he gets what he paid for. If he pays a high price for an outstanding meal, he does not mind the cost. But what is really perplexing is to pay a high price and still get a cheap meal!

Some waiters in a restaurant give patrons the unrelaxed feeling of standing right over them, smothering them, watching them eat, ready to grab the plate, or pour more water. At the other extreme, are those waiters who disappear, fail to notice the empty cup, and have to be flagged down to get any service.

Have you ever noticed how people stand in a line? If one stands too close to the person in front of him, he may seem pushy. If he stands too far back, people wonder if he is in line!

When we do business at the post office, market, or bank, if there is no conversation with the clerk, we may appear unfriendly. If we talk too much, the clerk may find

5

it difficult to do the necessary job. The ideal is a proper conversational balance.

A fine young Christian man I knew years ago, took a girl out to eat after church. She lived in a distant city and her pastor, who happened to know both of them, had arranged for them to meet. She was a nice looking Christian girl. But her personality was such that she had little to say. Conversation was difficult. He tried, but there was no exchange of thoughts, no communication. It was awkward. He never asked her out again.

MULTITUDE OF WORDS

At the other extreme, are those marathon talkers who try to monopolize every conversation, who constantly interrupt others, as though they know more than anyone else. "A fool's voice is known by multitude of words" (Ecc. 5:3). Their conversation is like the wind; it is difficult to tell from where it comes, or where it is going. They branch out, and branch out some more, seldom getting to a point. If they were to *write* the way they talk, periods would have to be replaced by commas! Some will say: "Oh I did not mean to do all the talking; I want to hear what *you* have to say"—and still *keep talking!*

The pastor of a Canadian church where I spoke several times, told me about a man he used to take home from church. As the man got out of the car, invariably he would be in the middle of a story. Standing by the car, he would place his elbows on the open window and continue talking. Not wanting to be impolite, the pastor would listen for a while. Finally, to give a hint, he would start moving the car forward. *Even then,* sometimes, this man would follow along, walking sideways, with elbows on the window— *still talking!* Poor man—maybe he was lonely. But the pastor was tired and wanted to get home!

It is with some hesitation I tell the following incident. Not far from the house where I grew up in Riverside,

6

California, we knew a woman that owned an orange grove. She was a good-natured, pleasant woman, but a non-stop talker. One evening she phoned a man who did tractor work in her grove. He had just come in from a long day's work as the phone rang. After answering, and finding out it was *her,* he laid the phone down. He needed to use the restroom! When he came back, she was still talking—never knew the difference!

Sometimes we all talk too much. We talk when we should listen. God gave us two ears, but only one tongue! "Let every man be swift to hear, slow to speak" (James 1:19). According to a saying attributed to Abraham Lincoln: "It is better to remain silent and be thought a fool, than to speak and remove all doubt." (cf. Proverbs 17:28).

POSITIVE THINKING

Positive thinking, rightly understood and in balance, is good. But having read *The Power of Positive Thinking,* when I saw a library book with the title *How To Cure Yourself of Positive Thinking,* I read it also. Each book makes valid points.

We tend to categorize people as positive or negative, as optimists or pessimists. But if the house is on fire and someone smells smoke, it is no time to be optimistic. It is not being negative to heed a warning. Fear is not always a negative—in some situations, it can keep us from falling off cliffs or being killed by driving recklessly.

Suppose a man believes it is impossible for his business to fail—because he believes in positive thinking. Then he goes out and spends money foolishly, buys equipment he does not need, an expensive car, an elaborate home, a boat, and uses charge accounts irresponsibility. Be assured that *positive thinking* is no substitute for *common sense.* He may fail financially, because he believes he *cannot* fail financially!

Another may positively believe no harm can come to him—so he refuses to buy insurance, doesn't wear a

7

seatbelt, and makes no provision for the future. He may not bother to make a will—after all, he's looking for the *Upper-taker,* not the *undertaker!* Someone may have a disease, but choose to believe he does not have it. His belief may be very positive, but neglecting treatment may only cause the disease to advance until it is incurable.

Some positive thinkers suppose that by concentrating hard enough, they can set up some cosmic energy to bring about an unrealistic objective. But why waste an entire life in frustration, trying to reach a goal that will never be reached? In spite of a few stories about people who faced adversity, beat the odds, and were successful—because they believed in themselves—there are multitudes that have believed they would become famous, would win a lottery, or attain greatness, and it never happened.

Suppose ten men in an election year are running for President of the United States. If each applies positive thinking, believing *he* will win, this will not make it happen. Only *one* person can become President. No matter how much an 80-year old woman tries to apply positive thinking, she is not going to win the 100-yard dash in the Olympics! Nor is she going to be "Miss America" in a beauty contest!

Paul said, "I can do *all things* through Christ who strengthens me" (Phil. 4:13). By naming and claiming this promise, can one obtain the finest home in town, drive the fanciest car, own an expensive yacht, and become rich? To the contrary, Paul had learned in whatever state he was in, to be content. He faced adversity and afflictions, yet he could endure all *these* things, because Christ gave him the strength to do so.

In Scripture, the expression "all things," often means "all [these] things"; that is, all things within the *context* in which the statement is made. For example, Paul wrote, "I have become *all things* to all men" (1 Cor. 9:22). In another place, he said, *"All things* are lawful for me" (1 Cor. 10:23).

8

An undue emphasis on the words *"all* things" in these verses, without the clarification of context, could lead to some wild conclusions!

Writing to a group of believers, John said the anointing taught them "all things," and consequently, they did not need "any man" to teach them (1 John 2:27). Some have quoted this verse, claiming that *God* speaks to them—that they don't need to listen to any *man!* But this cannot be the intended meaning, for God has clearly placed teachers in his church (Matt. 28:20; 1 Cor. 12:28; Eph. 4:11; 2 Tim. 2:24, etc.). The people to whom John wrote, understood "all [these] things"—the things within the context of which he was speaking. They needed no man to teach them these things.

If the people to whom John wrote knew *"all* things"— in a literal, absolute sense—we would have to conclude they knew the distance from the earth to the moon, how to build an airplane, and invent a computer!

ASK ANYTHING

Jesus said: "If you ask ANYTHING in my name, I will do it" (John 14:14). Some suppose this means they can ask for anything *they* want—all kinds of worldly possessions, riches, and fame. This was *not* what Jesus meant. The disciples, to whom he spoke these words, had a challenging and extensive mission ahead of them: to take the gospel into all the world. He promised to supply anything they would need—anything they would need to accomplish this purpose.

Consider this: The owner of a huge ranch, upon hiring a man to put up a fence along a remote part of his property, might tell him: "Here is a pickup truck you can use. It is loaded with fence posts, a large supply of wire, and various tools. Also, inside the truck is a cell phone. If you need *anything,* just call me and I will see that you get it." By "anything," he would obviously mean anything that would be needed, within the context of that conversation.

9

This is the way John—the one who recorded the "anything" promise of Jesus—understood it. He would later write: "If we ask ANYTHING *according to his will*...we know that we have the petitions that we desired of him" (1 John 5:14,15). It is *his* will—not our will—that is important. Let's face it, sometimes the things *we* want in life, may not be good for us.

On a bright sunny day, a boy was flying his kite. The kite said to the boy, "Give me more string, I want to go higher; it's beautiful up here!" The boy responded; still the kite kept crying out, "Give me more string, more string!" Finally the boy complained, "Kite, don't you know, the thing that holds you down, is the thing that holds you up?"

POVERTY / PROSPERITY

There was a time when some Christians seemed to glorify poverty. They figured a preacher, to be humble, should be poor. That was one extreme. But in time, with the upsurge of the economy, the pendulum has swung to the other extreme. Some now consider how well one does financially as a mark of God's favor. There is even talk that Jesus, were he here now, would drive a Rolls Royce!

There are "prosperity preachers" who suppose they should have the *best* of everything. Some attain these things—and, seemingly, an arrogance to match. To uphold these ideas, *many* biblical warnings must be ignored —like Paul's words:

"They that would be *rich* fall into temptation and a snare, and into *many* foolish and hurtful lusts, which drown men in destruction and perdition. For the love of money is the root of all evil: which while some coveted after, they have erred from the faith, and pierced themselves through with many sorrows" (1 Tim. 6:9,10).

Some folks see *dollar signs* when they read about prosperity in 3 John 2. It is as though *God* is saying to *them:* "Beloved, I wish above all things that you may PROSPER and be in health, even as your *soul* prospers." They take this to mean that God wants them to prosper *financially,* as much as he wants their soul to prosper *spiritually.* They fail to consider this was simply an introductory greeting in a letter from John to his friend Gaius, wishing him well.

The word that is here translated "prosper," has the meaning of "help on the road" (Strong's Concordance, 2137). In Romans 1:10 it is translated "have a prosperous journey." This was a common saying, also found other places in the Bible (Gen. 24:21,56; Josh. 1:8, Isa. 48:15). To have a prosperous journey simply meant that all would go well. This *might* involve finances, but that is not the primary meaning.

A popular fund raising method claims that people can GET, by giving. But this can easily get out of balance. If you plant corn, it is said, you will get corn; so if you plant money, you will get MONEY—lots of it. It sounds logical. But suppose one gives a large offering to a certain ministry. Having planted this seed, he will receive a crop of money—many times more than what he gave. He can then turn around and give more than before, and receive even more money! If this were true, Christians who practice seed giving would soon become the wealthiest people in the world!

We sometimes read great stories of famous people who believed in tithing, like John D. Rockefeller, who began tithing at age eight. Others include: James Kraft of Kraft Cheese, Henry Heinz of Heinz 57 Varieties, William Proctor of Ivory Soap, William Colgate of Colgate Shaving Cream, Matthias Baldwin of Baldwin Locomotive Industry, R. G. LeTourneau, manufacturer of heavy equipment, and J.C. Penney. All of these are to be commended for supporting Christian causes. They tithed and prospered. But, obviously, there are multitudes of very wealthy people who have founded or headed multi-million dollar companies, who did *not* tithe.

I know of a young man in our area that started to tithe and soon got a raise. His mother, who had encouraged him to start tithing, said, "See, God has blessed you for tithing!" "But, Mom," he said, *"everyone in the company got a raise!"*

Some ministries have "Prosperity Clubs" one can join by sending in offerings. Their promotional materials feature testimonies of people who gave to their ministry and prospered. But they never tell about all the ones that sent money that did *not* prosper. How honest is that?

Please do not misunderstand. We *strongly* believe that God blesses and rewards people for giving to his work—*of course!* There is no doubt about this, and the reward *may* involve finances. But that is not the complete picture. Often the greater blessings are *spiritual*—things like contentment, peace, and joy. James described Christians as "the *poor* of this world, but *rich in faith"* (James 2:5).

Support for the idea of "giving to GET" has been sought in the words of Jesus: "Give, and it shall be given unto you; good measure, pressed down, and shaken together, and running over" (Lk. 6:38). This has been taken to mean that by giving large offerings, people will get back so much money they will become rich, their bank accounts will be running over. This could hardly be the focus of Jesus' words, for he had just said, moments before: "Woe unto you that are rich!" (verse 24).

If we give because we love God and want to see the gospel go forward, this is the true motive. It is a *blessing* to give. "It is more blessed to give *than to receive"* (Acts 20:35).

But didn't the Philippians ask Paul how they could *receive* money in return for their giving? This is what some have preached! Paul's words in Philippians 4:15 are quoted: "When I departed from Macedonia, no church communicated with me concerning giving *and* RECEIVING, but you." But when this verse is studied in context, they wanted to know how they could give so *Paul* could receive money for his ministry! That was their concern.

Today, if some ask how we can receive an offering, we can give our mailing address. An offering can be given by check, money order, or credit card. We have email, telephone, and fax. It is not difficult to make contact. But back then it was not that easy. So the Philippians were concerned that Paul would receive what was sent. Paul mentioned he had received their previous offering that was brought to him by Epaphroditus.

Prosperity preachers may ask widows and poor people to give their last dime, as it were, promising that God will prosper them financially. One grows weary of hearing the story of Elijah and the widow's meal barrel used to justify this (1 Kings 17:8-16). That was a *unique* case. The church at Jerusalem practiced pure religion, seeing that widows were taken care of (Acts 6:1-4; James 1:27). There is no record that widows were told to give their last dime, and, by so doing, would get rich. Had this been the case, *they would not have needed the aid!* (cf. James 2:14-16).

It is humiliating to hear preachers beg for money, sometimes from poor and needy people, while they live in elaborate homes with lavish surroundings and drive exotic cars. "To them the Good News is just a means of making money. Keep away from them" (1 Tim. 6:5 *Living Bible* paraphrase). I wonder if they ever consider the little native preacher in a Third World country, who rejoices because God has supplied him a bicycle!

Let me hasten to say, for every preacher that has taken some financial advantage of the ministry, there are *many* that give heart and soul to the Lord's work, and do not receive large salaries. I have known literally hundreds of preachers over the years. Some work with their own hands to help keep the church doors open. They have a good retirement plan, though—it is "out of this world"!

It has been said, "There are three things that can ruin a preacher—popularity, money, and women." A preacher can become too popular and pride will hinder his effectiveness. On the other hand, unless he is popular enough to draw people to his church, he will have no one to preach to!

For every preacher that has been ruined by too much money, many have not had *enough* money to carry out the things they desire to do for God's work! Money is not wrong, it is the *wrong use* of money that is wrong.

Sometimes a preacher has been ruined by a woman. But in far more cases, a good wife has helped make a minister the man of God he is!

BOTH SIDES OF THE COIN

If a pastor drives a flashy, expensive car, it tends to raise questions about his priorities. What about the lost? Could money be spent more wisely? On the other hand, if he drives a wreck, he may not get where he needs to go. This could also discredit.

A minister should be friendly; yet professional. He should hold high standards; yet not have a "holier than thou" attitude (Isa. 65:5). His sermons should not be boring and uninteresting. Humor is not out of place, unless it is carried too far, and he acquires the image of a joke teller.

Some preachers are quick to expose sin, to cut and condemn, to render a guilty verdict, regardless of how many people they crush. They may quote Isaiah 58:1: "Cry aloud and spare not, lift up your voice like a trumpet and show my people their transgressions." But within that same chapter, are promises of healing for the hurting, water for the thirsty, food for the hungry, and satisfaction for the soul. Of course a stand should be taken against sin. But we should also place in the balance verses like:

"Speak evil of no man" (Titus 3:2).
"Be patient toward all men" (1 Thess. 5:14).
"Be gentle unto all men" (2 Tim. 2:24).
"We were gentle among you" (1 Thess. 2:7).
"Give no offence, neither to the Jews, nor to the Gentiles,
    nor to the Church of God" (1 Cor. 10:32).

14

One-sided preaching about how bad everything is getting, or how sinful people are, unless it is balanced with love and mercy, is like a surgeon who cuts open a body and fails to sew it up.

A young preacher (or an older one) may feel it is holy boldness if he can offend a lot of people. He is *sure* he is right. He can back up what he says with "proof text" verses. But in time, he may realize he has not weighed all the evidence. Others, equally sincere and godly, may have a basis for holding a different view. He begins to realize that truth is vast and that no one has unraveled all the mysteries of God.

CHOOSING A NEW PASTOR

A critical time in the life of a church is when a new pastor must be chosen. In some denominations he is appointed by the church hierarchy at headquarters, the local congregation having little or nothing to say about the decision. It is not a perfect system, and sometimes political maneuvering occurs. In other denominations, a congregational method may be used. Various preachers will come to "try out." During tryouts, the preacher, his wife, and children are all on display—everyone looking them over—deciding whom they will vote for. This is not a perfect system either!

A fine man I knew years ago, who attended a church where I spoke several times, told me they were having tryouts. The final vote had not happened yet, but he felt sure a certain man would get it. He really "preached hard against sin," he told me, "and played a guitar"! (He pronounced it GEE-TAR.) In many cases, someone less flashy—who would not do as well in a tryout situation—might have more spiritual depth and make a better pastor. I wonder how good the apostle Paul would have done?

Another method—casting lots—has occasionally been used to choose church leaders. The words "lot" and "lots"

15

appear about 100 times in the Bible—far more than commonly realized (Josh. 18:6; Proverbs 16:33; 18:18; Jonah 1:7). Matthias, who replaced Judas as one of the Twelve, was chosen by casting lots (Acts 1:23-26).

On a side note: we sometimes hear the view that Matthias was not *God's* choice—that *Paul* became the Twelfth Apostle. But Paul himself did not believe this way, for he wrote that Christ was seen after his resurrection by "the Twelve...and last of all he was seen of me also" (1 Cor. 15:5-9).

I heard about a pastor who took a church in a different state. Come to find out, the church had some overzealous board members who supposed they should tell everyone what to do, including the pastor. Because of some unforeseen delays, the new pastor, along with his family, arrived just in time for his first service. He went up on the platform, only to be told he was not to come on the platform until after the preliminaries. Probably with some fault on both sides, that pastor's first service was also his last—he resigned that morning! As they headed out of town, his son said to him: "Dad, the next time we go on vacation, do we have to take all the furniture with us?"

A story is told about a pastor who suffered strained relations with his congregation. He decided to take a job as Chaplain at the state prison. Many, elated he was leaving, turned out to hear his farewell sermon. He chose for his text: "I go to prepare a place for you...that where I am, there ye may be also" (John 14:2,3).

While there are many blessings that accompany ministry, dealing with people is not always easy. A pastor asked one of his members, "Aren't you concerned about all the *apathy* in our church?" The response was, "I don't know and I don't care."

In a restaurant, a man who had been a pastor in town for many years, was greeted with the words: "Good morning! How's the world treating you?" He thought a moment and replied, "You know, the world treats me pretty good—most of my problems are with the church folks!"

> Living with saints over there will be glory;
> Living with them here, is another story!

A minister is to be "the husband of one wife" (1 Tim. 3:2). This verse simply assumes that if he is married, he is to have one wife—he is not to be a polygamist. It does not mean a single man cannot be in the ministry. Paul was single. If a man's wife dies, leaving him without *any* wife, he is not disqualified from ministry.

A minister is to "rule well his own house, having his children in subjection...*for* if a man does not know how to rule his own house, how shall he take care of the church of God?" (1 Tim. 3:4,5). Seeking to obey this passage, there have been godly pastors who have quit the ministry—because of a rebellious son or daughter. But consider this: *God* certainly knew how to rule his own house, yet even HE had rebellious children: "I have nourished and brought up children, *and they have rebelled against me*" (Isa. 1:2).

We all know that Adam (who is called God's son—Luke 3:38), rebelled against him. These cases of rebellion did not cause *God* to quit being God! A pastor needs to know *how* to rule his own house, but this does not guarantee compliance. Again, balance comes into view.

The mention of a minister's *children* has caused some to ask: "Can a man who does not have children serve in a place of leadership? What if he has only *one* child? What if his children are adopted, do they count?" Questions like these, it seems to me, miss the point. Such verses simply assume he has children, and if so, how they are to behave. The father of John the Baptist, long before he had *any* children, served as a priest at Jerusalem (Lk. 1:5-7).

An evangelist we heard recently, told a story about three fathers-to-be that were waiting in the hospital maternity room. A nurse rushed in and congratulated one of the men—

his wife had just given birth to *twins*. He found this interesting—he played for the Twins baseball team! In a little while, a nurse came in and told the next man his wife had just given birth to *triplets!* He was amazed—he worked for the 3-M Company! About that time, the third man got up to *leave*. A nurse asked him if everything was alright. In a nervous voice he said, "I work for 7-UP!"

Occasionally there have been ministers who spend their whole life, as it were, saving others, while their *own* families are neglected. One pastor, seemingly very successful—speaking here, speaking there, heading this committee, promoting all kinds of good causes—actually experienced having his wife phone the church office, making an "appointment" to see him! Some who are always "too busy," need to organize their work and delegate responsibilities, as Moses' father-in-law told him to do (Exod. 18:18). No one is that indispensable. It is one thing to be *concerned,* another to be *paranoid!*

A woman told me once: "Since I got saved, I hardly clean house or cook meals for my family any more. I'm serving God!" We should not use God for an excuse. A family is a gift of God. Jesus expressed the principle of balance in these words: "...these ought you to have done, and not to leave the other undone" (Matt. 23:23).

Paul spoke of Epaphroditus, his associate, who *"for the work of Christ* was nigh unto death" (Phil. 2:25-30). He had overdone and suffered the consequences. He did recover, yet the wording, "God had mercy on him," falls short of implying a miraculous or instantaneous recovery. Though Paul had a healing ministry (Rom. 15:19), this did not replace a need for proper rest. Even Jesus came apart from the crowds—to be alone and pray. It has been said that if we do not come apart, we will "come apart."

At the other extreme, of course, are those in the ministry who are lazy. Isaiah described them as "dumb dogs, they cannot bark; sleeping, lying down, loving to slumber" (Isa. 56:10). What good is a non-barking, lazy, watchdog? God has called for *laborers* to work in his harvest (Matt. 9:37,38). The lazy approach—that if God wants it done, *he* will do it—is counterproductive. It is a privilege to be "workers together with him" (2 Cor. 6:1).

PHYSICAL FITNESS

Paul's statement to the young preacher Timothy, "Bodily exercise profits little" (1 Tim. 4:8), has sometimes been taken as a negative, as though he was against exercise. Not so. In context, what he was saying is that bodily exercise profits only for a little while—just in this life. So he encouraged Timothy to exercise himself unto godliness, which is beneficial now, *and* in the life to come.

Some get into physical fitness and exercise—it becomes almost an obsession with them; others do not exercise at all, are overweight, do not breathe deeply, seldom take a walk, and will use their car even when going a few hundred feet!

For good health, a person needs sunshine. But it is foolish to lie in the sun for hours to get a tan. Too much sunshine may cause skin cancer.

A clean air fanatic could advocate a law banning all cars from the highways—to clean up the unhealthy air. But then no one could drive. Some would protect beautiful wilderness areas to the extent that no roads could be built, effectively eliminating most people from seeing the areas they seek to preserve.

In Utah, Rainbow Bridge is the world's largest natural bridge—a marvelous sight to see. Because of its remote and rugged location, however, before Glen Canyon Dam was built, only a comparatively few brave souls ever ventured there. Now, because of the dam, it is accessible by tour boat, making it possible for many thousands to visit it each year.

In Yosemite National Park, walking from the parking lot toward Yosemite Falls, it is a spectacular sight to see water plunging 2,425 feet. Normally we would not want huge trees cut down in a protected area like this, but had this not been done, one could not see the falls for the trees!

If laws were passed to preserve all forests, what would we use for lumber? If we strip hills of all trees, we encourage erosion, and silt fills the rivers. Somewhere between the two extremes, is the practical balance.

If one catches all the fish from a lake, a renewable resource is depleted. Fishing, in balance, can provide food while still maintaining a supply.

The principle of balance makes a lot of sense!

A BALANCED MEAL

I like potatoes. I like fried potatoes, baked potatoes, mashed potatoes, boiled potatoes, potato soup, and potato chips. But a *balanced* meal will include more than potatoes! This is also true regarding our *spiritual* diet. Conclusions should not be based on one verse, when other verses will help provide a balanced meal.

This principle is well illustrated in the Temptation of Jesus. Satan, suggesting that he jump from a pinnacle of the Temple, quoted a scripture: "He shall give his angels charge concerning you: and in their hands they shall bear you up, lest at any time you dash your foot against a stone" (Psalms 91:11,12). But another verse, quoted by Jesus, provided the biblical balance: "Thou shalt not tempt the Lord thy God" (Deut. 6:16).

Truth must be based on the *total* testimony of Scripture, not an isolated verse out of context. As Jesus said, "Man shall not live by bread alone, but by EVERY word that proceeds out of the mouth of God" (Matt. 4:4; Deut. 8:3).

At a conference I attended years ago, two speakers sharply differed as to what the Bible teaches about the source of sickness. One claimed sickness is from SATAN.

He pointed out that it was Satan that smote Job with boils (Job 2:7), Satan caused a woman to be deformed for eighteen years (Lk. 13:11-16), and Jesus healed people who were "oppressed of the Devil" (Acts 10:38).

The other speaker argued that it is GOD who puts sickness on people. He pointed out that God put diseases on the Egyptians (Ex. 15:26), God took away Ezekiel's wife with a stroke (Ezek. 24:16-18), and God smote a king with leprosy (2 Kings 15:5). Thus one set of scriptures was pitted against the other. But the answer lies in accepting *both* sets of scripture, finding the biblical harmony.

Some churches advertise they are a "fun" church; that when they get together they have a good time! I have no doubt that the gatherings of the early Christians—people filled with the Holy Spirit and *joy* (Acts 13:52)—were victorious and upbeat. We believe in joy; yet sometimes joy, if not rooted in the Word, can be very shallow (Lk. 8:13). Along with the verses about joy, there are others that say "take up your cross," "through much tribulation we will enter the kingdom of God," "endure afflictions as a good solider," "the godly shall suffer persecution," etc. Just as some foods may not taste as good—but are actually *better for us*—so it is here. These verses must also be part of a balanced meal.

Even though large crowds followed Jesus, still—overall—only a "few" were finding the way to life eternal (Matt. 7:14). Was that a description of things as they stood at that time—or for all time? There are verses that speak of multitudes coming to Christ, singing his praise, worshipping him—wording that seems to imply more than just a "few" (Rev. 5:13; 7:9,10). Still other verses say that he is "the firstborn among *many* brethren," and that God will "bring *many* sons to glory" (Rom. 8:29; Heb. 2:10).

There are verses in the Bible that speak of God's wrath, anger, judgment, and condemnation. Other verses tell of his love, mercy, compassion, forgiveness, grace, and loving kindness. We do not have a balanced picture if one set of scriptures is quoted and not the other.

ETERNAL SECURITY?

Two viewpoints about the security of the believer—known in theological circles as Calvinism and Arminianism—have also produced two sets of scriptures.

"Calvinism," from John Calvin (1509 - 1564), holds that those who are truly converted can never be lost. This view, commonly called "eternal security," emphasizes scriptures about faith, grace, predestination, election, and God's sovereignty.

"Arminianism," from Jacobus Arminius (1560 - 1609), on the other hand, holds that some—though once converted—will be lost in the end. ("Arminianism" is not to be confused with Armenians, people of Armenia). This view, sometimes called "conditional security," emphasizes scriptures about repentance, Christian living, and man's responsibility before God.

Christians on the "eternal security" side believe we are saved by grace only; that we were chosen and elected in Christ before the foundation of the world. Our works, then, have nothing to do with us being saved, or keeping saved. Only those so elected will be drawn to Christ and those who are, will not be cast out. This glorifies God, it is believed, because its focus is not on what *we* do, but on what *he has already done.* It upholds his sovereignty. The following verses are quoted in support of this view:

God has "saved us, and called us...*not* according to our *works,* but according to *his own purpose and grace,* which was *given* us in Christ Jesus *before* the world began" (2 Tim. 1:9). "And if by *grace,* then it is no more of *works"* (Rom. 11:6).

"He has *chosen us* in him *before* the foundation of the world...having *predestinated us*...according to the good pleasure of *his will*...in whom we have redemption through

22

his blood...according to the riches of his *grace*...being *predestinated* according to the *purpose* of him who works all things after the counsel of *his own will*" (Eph. 1:4-7).

"For whom he did *foreknow,* he also did *predestinate*...them he also called; and whom he called, them he also justified: and whom he justified, them he also glorified...neither death, nor life, no angels, nor principalities, nor powers, nor things present, nor things to come, nor height, nor depth, nor any other creature, shall be able to separate us from the love of God" (Rom. 8:29-39).

Before Rebecca, Isaac's wife, gave birth to Jacob and Esau, "neither having done any good or evil, that the *purpose* of God according to *election* might stand, *not of works,* but of *him* that calls, it was said unto her, The elder shall serve the younger...I will have mercy on whom I will have mercy, and I will have compassion on whom I will have compassion. So then it is not of him that wills, nor of him that runs, but of *God* that shows *mercy*" (Rom. 9:11-16).

"*Elect* according to the *foreknowledge* of God...according to his abundant *mercy*" (1 Peter 1:2,3).

Jesus said: "No man can come to me, except the Father who has sent me draw him" (John 6:44). Does this sound like freewill? "*All* that the Father gives me *shall come to me;* and him that comes to me I will *in no wise cast out*" (verse 37). "*They* shall *never perish,* neither shall any man pluck them out of my hand" (John 10:28).

"*You* have not chosen me, but *I have chosen you,* and ordained you, that you should go and bring forth fruit, and that your fruit should remain" (John 15:16). "As many as were ordained to eternal life believed" (Acts 13:48). "The *Lord* added to the church daily such as should be saved" (Acts 2:47).

Prior to conversion, men are "*dead* in trespasses and sin" (Eph. 2:1). A dead man cannot save himself, so salvation must be entirely the work of him who is "the author *and finisher* of our faith" (Heb. 12:2). "He who has begun a good work in you, *will* perform [finish, complete] it" (Phil. 1:6). "The *grace* of God is *given* you by Jesus Christ...*who shall also confirm you unto the end,* that you may be blameless in the day of our Lord Jesus Christ" (1 Cor. 1:4-8).

CONDITIONAL SECURITY?

Christians who believe that eternal security is *conditional,* on the other hand, point out that while salvation is not by works, if one is truly saved, good works will follow. They point out numerous scriptural warnings—warnings seemingly without purpose if all believers are automatically and eternally secure. While God is sovereign, man must be responsible before God. The following verses are quoted in support of this view:

"We are not of them who draw back unto perdition, but of them that believe to the saving of the soul" (Heb. 10:39). Does not this imply "some" will draw back and their soul will not be saved?

"Brethren, if *any of you* do err [wander] from the truth, and one convert him: let him know, that he which converts [turns back] the sinner from the error of his way shall save a soul from death" (James 5:19,20). Would not this imply a Christian brother could wander from the truth, become a sinner, and his soul be lost?

Those who "escape the pollutions of the world through the knowledge of the Lord and Savior Jesus Christ," if they are again entangled therein, "the latter end is worse with them than the beginning. For it had been better for them not to have known the way of righteousness, than, after they have known it, to turn from the holy commandment delivered unto them" (2 Peter 2:20,21).

"For it is impossible for those who were once enlightened, and have tasted of the heavenly gift, and were made partakers of the Holy Spirit...if they shall fall away, to renew them again unto repentance; seeing they crucify to themselves the Son of God afresh, and put him to an open shame" (Heb. 6:4-6). If a person has repented, has been enlightened, has tasted the heavenly gift, has become a partaker of the Holy Spirit, are we to assume he never *really* came to Christ?

"He that overcomes...I will not blot his name out of the book of life" (Rev. 3:5). "Whosoever has sinned against me, him will I blot out of my book" (Exod. 32:33). Could a name be blotted out if it had never been there?

"To him that overcomes will I give to eat of the tree of life" (Rev. 2:7). "He that overcomes shall not be hurt of the second death" (verse 11). What about those who fail to overcome?

"He that *does the will of God* abides forever" (1 John 2:17). Would this not imply that if one does *not* do God's will he will *not* abide forever? "Not every one that says unto me, Lord, Lord, shall enter into the kingdom of heaven; but he that *does the will of my Father*" (Matt. 7:21).

Paul warned the Galatians against going back to Judaism, for then "Christ shall profit you nothing....Christ is become of no effect to you...you are *fallen from grace*" (Gal. 5:1-4). "Brethren, give diligence to make your calling and election sure: for *if* you do these things, *you shall never fall:* for so an entrance shall be ministered unto you abundantly into the everlasting kingdom of our Lord" (2 Peter 1:10,11). If it is impossible to fall, why these warnings?

Adam initially had fellowship and standing with God, yet we all know he fell. Angels that kept not their first estate fell (Jude 6). Branches that were once a part of God's olive tree, were cut off because of unbelief. "If God spared not the natural branches, *take heed lest he also not spare you*" (Rom. 11:20,21).

"The Lord, having saved the people out of the land of Egypt, afterward destroyed them that believed not" (Jude

5). "Now these things were our examples...wherefore let him that thinks he stands take heed *lest he fall*" (1 Cor. 10:11,12). "Take heed, *brethren,* lest there be in any of *you* an evil heart of unbelief, in *departing* from the living God" (Heb. 3:12). Can one depart *from* God if he has never come *to* God?

A number of "if" texts imply a conditional element: "...IF we hold fast the confidence and the rejoicing of the hope firm unto the end" (Heb. 3:6). "...IF you continue in the faith grounded and settled, and be not moved away from the hope of the gospel" (Col. 1:23). "...IF you keep in memory what I preached unto you, unless you have believed *in vain*" (1 Cor. 15:1,2).

GRACE / RESPONSIBILITY

Ironically, those who emphasize God's *grace* (Calvinism) and those who emphasize man's *responsibility* (Arminianism), sometimes quote from *the very same passages!*

Those who emphasize responsibility might quote Philippians 2:12: *"Work* out your own salvation with fear and trembling." But those who emphasize grace could point to the next verse: *"For* it is *God* who works in you both to will and to do of *his* good pleasure."

Those who emphasize grace might quote Ephesians 2:8, 9: "For by *grace* you are saved...not *works.*" But those who emphasize responsibility could point out the next verse: *"For* we are his workmanship, created in Christ Jesus *unto good works."*

Those who emphasize grace might quote Titus 2:11: "For the *grace of God that brings salvation* has appeared to all men." But those who emphasize responsibility could point out the verses that follow: "Teaching us that, denying ungodliness and worldly lusts, we should live soberly, righteously, and godly, in this present world...zealous of good works"!

Those who emphasize grace might quote Titus 3:5: *"Not by works of righteousness which we have done,* but according to his mercy he saved us." But those who emphasize responsibility could point out verse 8: "Be careful to maintain good works."

Those who emphasize grace might quote Hebrews 10:38: "The just shall live by *faith."* Those who emphasize responsibility could quote the rest of the verse: *"But* if any man draw back, my soul shall have *no* pleasure in him"!

Those who emphasize grace might quote John 6:37: *"All* that the Father gives me *shall come to me;* and him that comes to me I will *in no wise* cast out." But those who emphasize responsibility could quote verse 66: "Many of his disciples went back and *walked no more with him."*

Those who emphasize grace might quote Hebrews 5:8, that Christ is "the author of *eternal* [not temporary] salvation." But those who emphasize responsibility could quote the rest of the verse, that Christ is the author of eternal salvation "unto all who *obey* him."

Notice how God's grace, *and* man's responsibility, were intertwined by all these New Testament writers. This close proximity shows *they* did not see any conflict in these statements—and neither should *we!* If we would live "by every word of God," we should not pit one set of scriptures against another.

In his book *The Sovereignty of God* (p. 279), Arthur W. Pink has written:

> Two things are beyond dispute: God is sovereign, man is responsible.... That there is real danger of over-emphasizing the one and ignoring the other, we readily admit; yea, history furnishes numerous examples of cases of each. To emphasize the sovereignty of God, without also maintaining the accountability of the creature tends to fatalism; to be so concerned in maintaining the responsibility of man, as to lose sight of the sovereignty of God, is to exalt the creature and dishonor the Creator.

27

EXTREMES ON BOTH SIDES

Extremes, obviously, can develop on both sides, as the following examples show:

Jeffry had been raised in a Christian home and at a young age received Christ as his Savior. For years his whole live reflected spiritual values. But, when he was older, had suffered a painful breakup of his marriage, the loss of children, and business reverses, he began drinking heavily, his moral standards declined, and his life was a shambles. He readily acknowledged that he was not living for God, far from it! But, having been taught "once saved, always saved," he claimed he could not lose his salvation, only his reward.

Oscar was at the other extreme. He was taught that those who finally make it, will be saved by the skin of their teeth. Preaching in his church was sometimes so harsh, he often felt he must go to the altar and get saved again. It was as though God had a big club in his hand, just waiting for him to stray or make a mistake. It was like he was "saved" one day, "lost" another—bouncing back and forth. Surely there is more to salvation than a roller coaster experience like this!

Centuries ago, an overemphasis on works ultimately led to the Reformation. For many people, God's grace had become obscured by a maze of rituals. They were taught about Christ—even that he died for them and paid the price for their sins on the cross. But they must somehow strive to *merit* his grace. Over and over they must go and partake of the Mass. They must do penance and good works—always hoping for, but never quite sure, of salvation. Even in the hour of death they might need something more—the prayers of Mary on their behalf. Finally, through the cleansing fires of Purgatory, they hoped Heaven could be attained.

With the Reformation came a renewed emphasis on faith—"the just shall live by faith" (Rom. 1:17). If salvation were based on our works, there could be no real assurance of salvation. We could never be *good enough.* Yet, faith does not rule out works. Jesus said: "I know your works...because you are lukewarm I will vomit you out of my mouth" (Rev. 3:15,16). But works must be the result of faith, not the other way around.

Sometimes human thinking is inverted. We talk about "thunder and lightning," but actually it is lightning and thunder. We talk about "putting on our shoes and socks," but socks go on first! We talk about "going back and forth," yet how can one go back before going forth? Suppose we put a trailer in front of our car and attempted to push it to a distant city. How difficult it would be! But if the trailer *follows* the car, it is a different matter. So is it with faith and works. Faith is first; works follow.

One could hear Paul on faith—"A man is justified by faith without the deeds of the law" (Rom. 3:28)—and form a conclusion. Another could hear James on works—"By works a man is justified, and not by faith only" (James 2:24)—and form a different conclusion. But because both men were inspired, the truth must flow down the middle. There is a balance!

Even within the days of the early church, Paul's preaching about grace was misunderstood. Some supposed he was promoting laxness, even providing an excuse to sin. "We be slanderously reported, and as some affirm that we say, Let us do evil, that good may come" (Rom. 3:8). This, clearly, was not his position. "Should we continue in sin that grace may abound?" His answer: "God forbid!" (Rom. 6:1,2).

A man who once taught in a Bible College, said to me: "Any preacher who says a person has to DO anything, is false." I asked him how he would explain the Day of Pentecost when people, upon hearing Peter's message, asked: "What shall we *do?*" Peter did not reply: "You don't need to *do* anything!" No, he told them what to do—

to repent, to be baptized, and they would receive the gift of the Holy Spirit (Acts 2:38).

While it is true that prior to conversion we were "dead in trespasses and sins" (Eph. 2:1); and, obviously, there is nothing a dead man can do. But one should not press this analogy too far. A dead man cannot repent, yet God does command men everywhere to repent (Acts 17:30).

The idea that God's program is so inflexible there is nothing men can do, has even caused some to frown on missionary evangelism! A striking example involved the noted missionary William Carey (1761 - 1834). When he first spoke of going to India as a missionary, the elder John Ryland reportedly told him: "Sit down, young man. When God decides to save the heathen, He will do it without your help!"

In *Knowing the Doctrines of the Bible* (pp. 273,274), Myer Pearlman, has summed it all up in these words:

> The respective fundamental positions of both Calvinism and Arminianism are taught in the Scriptures. Calvinism exalts the grace of God as the only source of salvation—and so does the Bible; Arminianism emphasizes man's free will and responsibility—and so does the Bible.
>
> The practical solution consists in avoiding the unscriptural *extremes* of either view, and in refraining from setting one view in antagonism to the other. For when two Scriptural doctrines are set squarely in opposition to each other the result is a reaction that leads to error.
>
> For example: overemphasis on God's sovereignty and grace in salvation may lead to careless living, for if a person is led to believe that his conduct and attitude have nothing to do with his salvation, he may become negligent. On the other hand, overemphasis of man's free will and responsibility, in reaction against Calvinism, may bring people under the bondage of legalism and rob them of all assurance. Lawlessness and legalism—these are the two *extremes* to be avoided.

When Finney ministered in a community where grace had been overemphasized he bore down heavily on the doctrine of man's responsibility. When he held a meeting in a community where human responsibility and works had been stressed, he emphasized the grace of God. And as we leave the mysteries of predestination and set ourselves to the practical task of getting people saved, we shall not be troubled by the matter. Wesley was an Arminian and Whitefield was a Calvinist. Yet both led thousands to Christ.

Godly Calvinistic preachers of the type of Spurgeon and Finney have preached the perseverance of the saints in such a manner as to discourage carelessness. They were careful to point out that while a true child of God was certain to persevere to the end, the fact that he did not so persevere would put in question the fact as to whether he had really been born again! If a person did not follow after holiness, said Calvin, he would do well to question his election.

It is not uncommon for a congregation to have some who believe one way and some the other. Is believing in eternal security—or *not* believing in eternal security—so important that a church should split over it? So many times people feel obligated to wave one banner or the other. I would suggest a third position, as it were: Find the biblical balance by avoiding the *extremes* on both sides, accept the *scriptures* on both sides, and accept *each other* as members of the family of God.

BELIEVING *ONE* THING

People lose balance by believing one thing—even though there is some truth in it—to the exclusion of other things. Like one who stares at a bright light: its very brightness can have a blinding effect.

My long-time friend, Pastor Jim Westbrook, has pointed out that balance and extremism are like oil and water: they just won't mix. Down through history, the Holy Spirit has brought truths to light from the Word. These truths

31

have been a blessing. But when people emphasize *one* truth above all other previously known truths, the lack of balance may cause it to be ineffective, like yesterday's manna.

I knew a pastor who came to a different—and, in my opinion, a *better*—understanding of Bible prophecy. But he became dogmatic about it, seldom preaching on anything but prophecy, causing division. In one year, his church went from 200 people to 20. He left and someone else had to pick up the pieces.

Sometimes it is what people *do* with a doctrine—more than the doctrine itself—that causes needless splits and splinters among the people of God.

THE SACRED NAME

This has certainly been the case, in my opinion, with the "Sacred Name" doctrine. This is the teaching that the Hebrew name of the Heavenly Father—YHWH—commonly translated LORD or JEHOVAH, should really be translated YAHWEH.

I was 20 years old when I first heard about this teaching. While walking along a deserted ocean beach in San Diego (it was winter time), I prayed about it. I wrote the letters YHWH in the sand and pondered: Would prayer be more powerful if I used this name? Would my ministry be more effective if I no longer used words like Lord or God—using Yahweh instead?

With all due respect to some very fine, sincere people who believe this way, with the passing of years, I must say I have never seen this teaching produce any real spiritual fruit. If the Heavenly Father were putting some special blessing on those that use the name Yahweh—and if those who use words like Lord or God were *not* blessed by him— the evidence would be clear.

They were a nice family—father, mother, and three children. All were regular in their church attendance and active evangelical Christians. Then the father began to study Sacred Name literature. He dropped out of church, believing that all the churches in their community—because they did not exclusively use the name Yahweh—were actually worshipping Baal. The name "Jesus," he concluded, was but another form of Zeus, a pagan god.

It became quite an issue in their home. It wasn't long until none of them went to church anymore. Versions of the Bible that use words like "God," "Lord," and "Jesus" were abhorred. Hymns about Jesus that once rang out in their hearts, were now scorned. Great preachers and reformers in history, some who gave their lives for their faith, were no longer esteemed. As the children grew up and married, all married outside the church, with little or no faith remaining. Such are the fruits of extreme teachings.

Tiny Sacred Names groups are often divided among themselves, even on how to spell the Heavenly Father's name. With several of their publications in front of me, here are some of the variations: Yahweh, Yahvah, Yeve, Yeheveh, Yehueh, Yehovah, YawHooh, or Yahuwah. There are also those who use the name Jahweh in various forms. But most Sacred Name people don't like the letter J (as in Jesus or Jehovah), so Jeremiah becomes Yeremyah, Joel becomes Yahyl, John becomes Yahchanan, Jerusalem becomes Yerushalem, etc.

Some complicate things even more by supposing their own names should be changed. Someone with a name like Jim—a name that is easy to spell and pronounce—may be changed to something like Yimhozzyiel.

Of all the Sacred Name believers I have known over the years, I have yet to meet even *one* whose conversion came through the efforts of a Sacred Name church. All were converted in some *other* church and the Sacred Name belief came later. Why are these churches unable to win souls? Could it be that an overemphasis on technical points has hindered the flow of the Holy Spirit?

Be assured, the Heavenly Father does have a name. That name, referred to as the tetragrammaton—YHWH— appears over 6,000 times in the Old Testament. Even Jehovah's Witnesses admit, as in the preface of their *New World Translation of the Scriptures,* that "Jehovah" is probably not the best translation. Most translations use LORD, putting it in capital letters to indicate Deity.

Jewish people have long felt the actual name is too sacred to pronounce. In English, it is difficult to know which vowels should be added to the letters YHWH. If some believe that "Yahweh" is the correct spelling, I have no problem with this. But let's not destroy the work of God over it.

WIVES IN SUBMISSION

There are teachings about "submission" that have sometimes been carried to a hurtful extreme. Some have taught that a wife must obey her husband, even if it means following him into sinful living. If he wants her to go to bars with him, she should go. If he tells her to lie, she should lie. This is false.

So often verses are quoted about a wife being in subjection to her husband, yet the Bible also says *"all of you are to be subject one to another"* (1 Peter 5:5; Eph. 5:21).

It is one thing for a husband to take a place of responsibility for his family; it is another thing to suppose God wants him to be a *dictator.* This could not be what Paul meant, for he said, "Husbands, *love* your wives, *even as Christ loved the church"!* (Eph. 5:25). Men who have the attitude, "It's MY way or the highway," can rob a home of peace and happiness.

Picture a woman who is married to a man who is irresponsible, spends money foolishly, getting the family deeper and deeper in debt. Some would have us believe "submission" requires her to say nothing. But wait! If he dies or deserts, she may end up with all of those bills; *she* could be held legally responsible; she will be the loser.

Sarah, Abraham's wife, is mentioned as an example of a woman being in subjection to her husband (1 Peter 3:5,6). But this did not mean she could not express her opinion. On at least one occasion, God told Abraham to listen to his wife! "And God said unto Abraham...in all that Sarah has said unto you, hearken unto her" (Gen. 21:12).

Despite the extremism of some women's rights activists, they are not wrong on everything. Over the centuries, women have suffered untold cruelty at the hands of men. To this day, in some countries, women must keep their faces hidden behind a veil, sexual mutilation has been forced on them, they are considered unclean, are not allowed to vote, or drive a car.

There are four verses that basically say: "Wives, submit yourselves unto *your own* husbands" (Col. 3:18; Eph. 5:22; 1 Peter 3:1,5). In each instance, it was their "own" husbands they were to be submitted to—not someone else's husband, not a man down the street. The very wording implies, primarily, *moral* faithfulness. *We* might read over this point, assuming wives would *automatically* know they should be true to their husbands. But many of these early converts had come from pagan backgrounds and moral issues that *we* might take for granted, needed clarification.

At the other extreme, some of the Corinthian Christians, living in a city known for its immorality, questioned if sexual union—even in marriage—was proper. Some were married to unbelievers. Were they required to break up their marriages? Would children born to these unions be "unholy"?

Paul answered this way: A Christian was not required to leave an unbelieving mate, but if the unbeliever left, a Christian was no longer bound. Children born to marriages between believers and unbelievers were not unholy. Except in cases where some desired a single life, every man was to have his own wife and every woman her own husband. Sexual union was not forbidden, except by mutual consent during times of prayer and fasting (1 Cor. 7:2-5, 14,15).

Some churches take such an extreme stand against divorce, a woman may believe she has to stay with an unfaithful husband "no matter what." But if she contracts AIDS from him, dies, and leaves behind little children, how is God glorified in this? People need to avoid extreme teachings that bring them into bondage.

If a teaching seems weird or unbalanced, it probably is!

GOD'S PERFECT WILL

Ed and Jane believed it was "God's perfect will" for them to get married. But before they said, "I do," Jane met another man, fell in love, and married him. So, assuming she married outside the will of God, where does this leave Ed? If he marries someone else, will he be forever outside God's will? We think not. God's will is vast, and is not frustrated by the folly of people.

A church had invited a young preacher to come hold special meetings. He assumed it was God's will for him to do so—after all, he didn't have any *other* invitations. While there, he received another invitation. Then more invitations came—each seemingly indicating God's will and direction for him. But as the Lord blessed his ministry and he became better known, he received more invitations than he could accept. He could not be five places at the same time! Thus, it would seem, his initial premise was not necessarily the way to determine God's will.

We have heard people say—perhaps upon returning from a trip: "We knew we were in the will of God—everything went *smoothly,* there were no problems of any kind!" We rejoice when things go smoothly; but this, in itself, does not indicate one is in the will of God. The

Israelites were following God's will when they came out of Egypt, yet they found themselves between the Devil and the deep Red Sea! Paul certainly functioned within the will of God, yet things did not always go smoothly for him. Jesus, who *always* did the will of the Father, was crucified!

On the other hand, just because people have trouble does not indicate they are in the will of God, either. Many factors enter in. If a person's life is out of balance, if he makes stupid decisions and brings about unnecessary trouble, he should not use this as proof he is in God's will.

It would be a great gift to always have divine guidance. I have not attained it and I don't know anyone who has. Haven't we all made some bad decisions—made a car purchase we later regretted, made a poor investment, or trusted the wrong person?

HEARING GOD'S VOICE

Does God speak to people today? I believe he does; but there have been some unfruitful extremes. Without judging her sincerity, I knew of a woman years ago who claimed God talked to her a lot, even revealing recipes to her. But another woman, who had eaten some of her cooking, told me: "If God gave her that recipe, he is not a very good cook!"

There are others who use all kinds of coincidences—sometimes in superstitious ways—as messages from God. "I phoned this woman; at that very moment she picked up—this must be God!" One fellow said, "God is telling me to go to Richard's house—right now!" But when he got there, Richard was not home. Was this really God's message to him?

After speaking at a church in New York—when nearly everyone had left—a young man came back behind the platform and asked me: "Is there a Susan Johnson that attends this church?" I explained that I did not know, but he could ask the pastor who was in an adjoining room. The pastor said there was no one by that name that attended services there. The young man, somewhat puzzled, said: "I don't understand, *God* told me to come to this church tonight, that I would meet my wife-to-be, that her name is Susan Johnson."

Despite unfortunate extremes like this, I am not in the camp of those who say God never speaks to anyone, anymore. But, when it is God, I believe it will prove out and be fruitful. I believe he can speak in many ways, directly or indirectly. He can speak through the Bible, preachers, circumstances, and even dreams.

In the Scriptures, God spoke in dreams to people like Jacob, Solomon, and Daniel (Gen. 31:11; 1 Kings 3:5; Dan. 7:1-14). Sometimes he even used dreams to speak to people who did not know him, like King Nebuchadnezzar and Pilate's wife (Dan. 2:1-49; Matt. 27:19). Jesus' conception was explained to Joseph in a dream and, later, after Jesus was born, about the need to flee into Egypt (Matt. 1:20; 2:13). Visions and dreams were among the blessings included in the outpouring of the Holy Spirit on the day of Pentecost (Acts 2:17).

The Bible also warns about dreams that are not of God (Deut. 13:1-5). Some dreams, neither good nor evil, stem from our own thoughts, consciously or otherwise (Ecc. 5:3,7). Every dream, obviously, is not a message from God! Two examples will suffice:

A friend of mine once told me how his uncle, a preacher, dreamed he would be called to pastor a large church. There he would have a remarkable ministry. He believed the dream would happen soon, because, in the dream, he was driving a Hudson, the car he owned at that time. Years passed; the Hudson was getting old and undependable. But he would not sell it, because in the dream *he was driving that Hudson!* Finally, lack of fulfillment, forced him to conclude his dream was not a message from God.

When I was perhaps 15 years old, seeking God's will for my life, I dreamed a man came to our door and handed me a box. When I opened it, inside was a smaller box, which also contained a smaller box, etc. When all were finally opened, there was only a slip of paper with a Scripture reference written on it: "Galatians 3:31." I immediately awoke, thinking God was telling me something. I reached for my Bible on the nightstand, only to find *there is no Galatians 3:31!*

On the positive side, I believe God's hand has been on my life; I believe he has guided me in different ways—but this particular incident was not one of them!

SOUL WINNING CAMP

About this same time in my life, a very fine woman in our church in Riverside, California, encouraged me to go to a three-week soul winning camp, and even paid my way. The total price: $25! This not only included the camp itself, food, and lodging, but transportation—we were bused from Los Angeles to a huge ranch out in the middle of nowhere, near Mingus, Texas. There, in primitive living conditions, we were drilled day and night in soul winning tactics.

Being young and impressionable, we were in awe as one of the leaders told of his bold witnessing exploits. Perhaps the most bizarre was how he and another man had gained entrance to a movie theater using what looked like tickets, but which were really printed Bible verses. Once inside, he got everyone's attention by hollering out: "Fire! Fire!" The other man, in a different part of the theater, responded: "Yes, there's fire in Hell, and you are going there unless you repent!"

Years later, I would read that "to shout 'fire!' in a crowded theater," was a phrase used by Supreme Court Justice, Oliver Wendell Holmes, to illustrate there are limits to freedom of speech. But we knew nothing about such things at the time.

One of the camp leaders told how he had been drafted into the army. He showed up at the induction center with his Bible and witnessed to everyone he met, regardless of rank. He was sent to the army psychiatrist, to whom he also witnessed. He was soon dismissed! On his car, he had an upward-facing sign on the roof—"Jesus Saves"—presumably so people in airplanes would see it!

We were stirred—it seemed God was telling each of us: "Go YE into all the world and preach the gospel to EVERY creature" (Mark 16:15). This meant, we supposed, that we were to aggressively witness to every single person, regardless of when or where! To put what we were being taught into practice, we were taken into downtown Ft. Worth, Texas, to work the streets.

Usually two of us would be paired, one who was more experienced with one who was less experienced. In the incident I am about to relate, the young man I was with, was more experienced—I believe his name was John—so he took the lead. We approached a man standing in the open doorway of a liquor store, apparently the owner.

John asked him if he were to die that night, would he go to Heaven or Hell. (It was a very hot August day in Ft. Worth, which seemed to make a question about Hell especially relevant!).

"How are you so sure there is a Hell?" he asked.

"The *Bible* says so!"

"Oh, I see," the owner of the liquor store calmly answered. "You boys read that in a book, the Bible. Well, I have a book in here that I'm reading. It says Hell is not as hot as it used to be—they have recently put in a big air conditioning unit down there!"

Sometime part of our group might be on one side of a downtown street, and the other across the street. One side would holler out, in cheer-leader fashion, "Hey kids—what's John 3:16?" They would respond by hollering out the words of the verse. When we did this in front of bars or theaters, we supposed we were really giving the Devil a black eye.

Despite some of these extremes, in many ways the soul winning camp was a positive experience. It helped me overcome some of my timidity. It was on the bus going to the camp I met a lifelong friend, Fred Horner, who has had a fruitful ministry over the years as a pastor and missionary in several countries.

But, in time, we came to see that some of the soul winning methods we were taught, lacked balance. If our witnessing methods constantly offend people, discredit us as religious fanatics, or give others the wrong impression, we miss the mark. If people get the feeling someone is trying to high-pressure them into something, their barriers are immediately up.

When Jesus said, "Go ye into all the world and preach the gospel to every creature," he was speaking to those he had chosen to be his apostles. I have always been missionary-minded; I believe every Christian, in one way or another, should have a part in spreading the gospel. But, Jesus was not telling *every* Christian to go into all the world and preach! If *every* Christian became a missionary, who would be left to provide support?

And, Jesus' words to the apostles about preaching to "every creature"—meaning people of all nations, colors, and cultures—can hardly justify the teaching that every Christian is to literally witness to *every* person he comes in contact with, immediately, and on the spot.

Two young men, who were attending a Bible school, had part-time jobs at a sporting goods store. They tried to "witness" to every customer that came in! When the boss reprimanded them, they felt they were being *persecuted!* But a minister connected with the Bible school—a relative of mine—told them they should *quit* witnessing on the job. He wisely pointed out that the boss was not paying them to preach, but to sell sporting goods!

41

Back in the 1960s, a woman told me she was thinking of having red splotches painted all over her white station wagon to look like blood, and a large sign with the words: "The blood of Jesus Christ cleanseth from all sin" (1 John 1:7).

On a busy downtown San Francisco sidewalk, I have observed a man walking back and forth with a sign suspended from his shoulders, front and back:

BABYLON THE GREAT IS FALLEN, IS FALLEN, AND IS BECOME THE HABITATION OF DEVILS. ALL NATIONS HAVE DRUNK OF THE WINE OF HER FORNICATION. COME OUT OF HER, MY PEOPLE" (REVELATION 18:2-4).

Though cities like San Francisco may be modern "Babylons," and though it is true the blood of Jesus cleanses from all sin, if our tactics place us in the "nut" category, they will not be very effective.

When I was 21 years old, while holding meetings in Porterville, California, someone directed me to a Christian barber. As I got into the chair, I introduced myself, and the barber was thrilled to learn I was a preacher. With enthusiasm he showed me the method he used to witness.

First he turned the chair one direction where a customer could not fail to see a sign on the wall: "And the smoke of their torment ascendeth up for ever and ever..." (Rev. 14:11). This became the text for the first part of his sermon! As the customer was turned in the chair, he faced another verse, similar in nature to the first, and the message continued. He didn't beat around the bush. Sin was black, Heaven was high, and Hell was hot!

By the time he had the straight-edged razorblade in his hand, he was really excited, jerking and waving his hand around, praising the Lord! I felt uneasy, and I was a *preacher!* I wondered about the poor sinner who might venture into this place! I did get a good haircut, and was not charged any extra for the sermon!

The Bible speaks of some who have "a zeal for God, but not according to knowledge" (Rom. 10:2). Nevertheless, let me hasten to say: for every Christian that may go overboard, I fear there are MANY that never speak up at all. That extreme must *surely* be avoided.

The story is told about a young Christian man who got a job working in a remote logging camp for the summer. Knowing he would be among many ungodly men, the church back home continually held him up in prayer. They knew it could be rough for him as he shared his Christian testimony. At the end of the summer, when he returned, they asked him how he had survived during this time, because of his stand as a Christian. "Oh just fine," he replied, *"they never found out!"*

While *every* Christian should let his light shine, should share his faith with others, should be a witness, not all have the *same* gift (Rom. 12:6). Some who grew up in ungodly homes, who lived a life of sin and rebellion against God, when converted, may be better soul winners than some raised in a Christian home. Often they can better relate to sinners; they have been there and done that.

Each of us—as Paul on the road to Damascus—should pray: "What will you have *me* to do?" Each of us, not allowing fear to hold us back, should stir up the gift that is within us (2 Tim. 1:6,7). If that gift is soul winning, great! But if this is not our primary gifting, we should not live in condemnation because we are not personally winning hundreds of souls to Christ. Some may plant the seed, another may water, but God gives the increase (1 Cor. 3:5,6).

We like instantaneous conversions—right now and on the spot. But some conversions come about more gradually. For example, one woman was a Christian; her husband was not. But, he was willing to come to church with her and the children. Week after week he heard the Word lovingly presented. Like seed, it began to find lodging in

43

his heart. Eventually he blossomed into a dynamic, vibrant believer. Patience on the part of the pastor and congregation paid off.

In contrast to this case, I knew a man who went to a revival meeting many years ago. When the invitation was given for sinners to receive Christ, several tried to pressure him into going forward. When he refused, two of them even tried to pick him up and carry him forward! They had a lot of zeal, they meant well, but this man was so deeply embarrassed and offended, he never went back to church.

It is bad enough in the secular world when a person is pushy. People often find it even more aggravating when they feel someone is trying to push a *religious* belief off on them. A man convinced against his will, is of the same opinion still. Witnessing to others is a good thing. But if we do a good thing in a wrong way, we blemish the point we would make. The principle, "Except the *Lord* build the house, they labor in vain that build it," might well apply here (Psalms 127:1).

While God uses *people* to preach the gospel, it is still the Holy Spirit that convicts and converts. When Peter preached on the Day of Pentecost, those who *"gladly* received his word" were baptized (Acts 2:41)—no one was *forced* into religious commitment.

We would certainly oppose laws *forbidding* prayer—in public schools or anywhere else—but we would also oppose laws *forcing* prayer on anyone. Prayer, in the true sense, must come from the heart. If schoolteachers were required to lead prayers, in some cases we would have non-believers praying prayers. There might be Roman Catholic prayers, Mormon prayers, Pentecostal prayers, or Baptist prayers—none of which have anything to do with reading, writing, and arithmetic. The three Rs (as they are called) are, after all, non-denominational.

Sometimes people will "bomb" the parking lot of a church with which they differ—placing literature on cars.

(Regretfully, a couple times, people have done this with articles *I* have written!) But because most regard this as unethical behavior, a form of trespassing, and in poor taste, the point being made—even if valid—is rendered ineffective.

One man said, "I never leave a big tip for the waitress, but I always leave her a gospel tract." This would be all the more reason to leave a good tip!

CHURCH CONTESTS

As a young preacher, in 1959, I held evangelistic meetings at a church in St. Joseph, Missouri. The church was in the middle of a three-month contest, aimed at getting their people to witness to neighbors and friends, inviting them to church. The prize was a 1952 Chevrolet coupe, someone had donated. Parked right in front, it had a then-popular windshield visor, a two-tone paint job, and some sharp-looking hubcaps. The pastor told me one woman, in her effort to win the car, had already brought *over 100 new people to church.* Another was running a close second!

The pastor went on to tell me his method for building the Sunday School. "Each child that brings a new boy or girl, I personally hand him a silver dollar," he told me. "Each week I give out 30 to 50 silver dollars. A display ad in the newspaper would cost about the same, with little or no results. I'd rather give the money to the kids!"

Contests had seemingly worked well for this church, yet the pastor told me right out: "I know people ought to do it for Jesus, not to win a prize." I have never been big on contests. But, I must tell you that we know people who are serving the Lord today, because, years ago, someone invited them to church as part of a contest. Again, balance is in order.

I heard a pastor at a conference tell about "dumb things" (to use his term) that have been done to get people to attend church. He told how he once went to a barbershop and got a bunch of hairs. These were then mailed in envelopes, along with the message: "I am tearing my hair out—wanting so bad to see you in church!"

JEHOVAH'S WITNESSES

We do not always agree with the witnessing methods used by the Jehovah's Witnesses; but, to their credit, they do witness. Christians of a more evangelical persuasion, commonly regret seeing people swayed by them. But, to some extent, this would not be the case, if *they* had done more witnessing.

In our area, Jehovah's Witnesses set up a table displaying their literature in front of a supermarket. I suppose this is considered freedom of speech, and so it is permitted. But if it were turned around, would they want the supermarket setting up a table at the entrance of their Kingdom Hall to sell magazines, American flags, Christmas ornaments, and other things they do not agree with?

If an organization were to set up a table offering literature about health problems, it would *seem* like a good service. *But,* if that information is unreliable, it could be deadly. This is a problem with the Jehovah's Witnesses. They are not wrong on "everything"—within their numbers are fine, sincere people, some I know personally. But the claim that their organization, and no other, teaches what the Scriptures say, is misleading. It takes people on a spiritual detour.

Years ago I read the six volumes, *Studies in the Scriptures,* written by their founder, Charles Taze Russell (1852 – 1916). He says some good things in these books, but other information is so flawed, even the present-day Witnesses no longer promote his books.

Jehovah's Witnesses have built their organization by pointing out errors, real or imagined, in the older, established denominations. Yet many of these denominations have built hospitals, operate orphanages, and provide massive food relief to famine stricken countries—far beyond anything ever done by the Jehovah's Witnesses. What is pure religion? "Pure religion and undefiled before God and the Father is this, To visit the fatherless and widows in their affliction, and to keep himself unspotted from the world" (James 1:27). Pure religion is practical and goes beyond mere doctrinal differences, whether spoken or in print.

ARGUMENTS FROM SILENCE

We sometimes hear the claim: "Where the Scriptures speak, we speak; where the Scriptures are silent, we are silent." While not a bad saying in itself, a biblical balance is certainly in order. We should not assume something is wrong simply because there is a silence of Scripture!

By this method one could argue against the use of song books, black-cover Bibles, dividing the Bible into chapters and verses, Bible colleges, printing presses, individual communion cups, church buildings, baptismal tanks, sound systems, air conditioning, church buses, radio or television programs, and a host of other things!

If a practice were wrong simply because of scriptural silence, we would not need any "thou shalt not" verses in the Bible. It would only need to give positive commands. We would then know that *everything else* is wrong—*automatically*—because of silence. It was this kind of reasoning that caused people in one small group to abstain from eating tomatoes or potatoes—because these words "are not mentioned in the Bible"!

About a century ago, it was basically an argument from silence that caused the restoration movement of Alexander Campbell to split. The issue: musical instruments. The non-musical side, using the name Church of Christ, opposed the use of musical instruments because they are not mentioned in the New Testament.

I have known a number of people who belong to this church, including a medical doctor, two pastors, some relatives, and neighbors. I have no reason to doubt their faith in Christ. But having said this, and with all due respect, I do not believe their argument against musical instruments is very strong.

MUSICAL INSTRUMENTS

It is acknowledged, on all sides, that musical instruments were commonly used in the *Old* Testament, as in the following examples:

Beginning in Genesis, we read about musicians who played the harp and organ (Gen. 4:21). In Exodus, Miriam and others played timbrels (tambourines) as they sang praises to God (Exod. 15:20-21). The women singers of Israel were accompanied with "instruments of music" (1 Sam. 18:6). The prophet Elisha asked that a musician be brought to him. "As *he played,* the hand of the Lord came upon him," and he began to prophesy (2 Kings 3:15,16; cf. 1 Sam. 10:5).

David played a harp, and appointed people to be "singers with instruments of music, psalteries [stringed instruments], harps and cymbals" (1 Sam. 16:23; 1 Chron. 15:16). Toward the end of his life, among the priests and Levites, there were 4,000 that praised the Lord with musical instruments (1 Chron. 23:5). In the Psalms— many written by David—the harp, trumpet, cornet, psaltery, a ten-stringed instrument, and others, are mentioned in worship settings (Psalms 33:2; 98:5,6).

During Solomon's reign, at the dedication of the Temple, they used "cymbals and psalteries and harps, trumpeters and singers...praising and thanking the Lord...and the glory of the Lord filled the house of God" (2 Chron. 5:12-14).

Isaiah wrote about singing, accompanied by "stringed instruments all the days of our life in the house of the Lord" (Isa. 38:20). Hezekiah "set the Levites in the house of the Lord with cymbals, with psalteries, and with harps...for so was *the commandment of the Lord* by his prophets" (2 Chron. 29:25).

Despite these *many* verses, some have quoted one verse—about a rebellious people "that chant to the sound of the viol, and *invent to themselves instruments of music like David"* (Amos 6:5).

The rebellious people Amos referred to in this verse—like David—used musical instruments. But David used them in the worship of God; they used them as a part of their debauchery and idolatry. The instruments were not evil—the wrong use of them was evil. The Bible mentions "the musical instruments of David *the man of God"* (Neh. 12:36)—strange wording, if musical instruments were evil.

Doubtless, musical instruments were a part of *Old* Testament worship, and were even commanded by the Lord. The question is: Did this change in the *New* Testament?

As I understand it, the basic argument against instrumental music is this: "The New Testament says to worship the Lord with *singing;* it is *silent* about the use of musical instruments. So, *only* singing is proper in church."

But the rule of *silence* must have its limitations. If musical instruments are wrong because the New Testament is silent about their use, this could work the other way, too. The New Testament is also silent about any command *not* to use them! Because musical instruments had an established use in the Old Testament, it could be argued that the silence of any New Testament command *changing* this usage, might be the weightier of the two.

But is the New Testament silent about the use of musical instruments?

An often-quoted verse about the importance of singing is Ephesians 5:19: "Speaking to yourselves in psalms and hymns and spiritual songs, singing and *making melody* in your heart to the Lord." It is our understanding that the words "making melody" (as in the King James version), refer to the use of musical instruments. Consider the following translations of this portion:

MOFFATT: "Praise the Lord heartily with words *and* MUSIC."

BERKELEY: "Singing heartily *and* MAKING YOUR MUSIC to the Lord."

TWENTIETH CENTURY: "Sing *and* MAKE MUSIC in your hearts to the Lord."

NEW ENGLISH BIBLE: "Sing *and* MAKE MUSIC in your hearts to the Lord."

NEW INTERNATIONAL VERSION: "Sing *and* MAKE MUSIC in your heart to the Lord."

In these translations, "singing" is one thing; "making music" is another—and both are to be done from the heart, heartily. Some translations, as the following, are stronger yet:

AMPLIFIED: "Offering praise with voices (*and* IN-STRUMENTS) making melody with all your heart to the Lord."

BALLENTINE: "Singing *and* PLAYING THE HARP heartily to the Lord."

BECK: "And with your heart sing *and* PLAY MUSIC to the Lord."

CONCORDANT: "Singing *and* PLAYING MUSIC in your hearts to the Lord."

ROTHERHAM: "Singing *and* STRIKING THE STRINGS with your heart unto the Lord."

But we need not be dependent only on *translations.* We can go right to standard reference works like *Strong's Concordance* and look up the Greek definitions. The term "making melody" in Ephesians 5:19 is translated from *psallo,* meaning: "to twitch or twang, i.e. *to play on a stringed instrument*" (Strong's Concordance, 5567).

Psallo, in turn, is based on *Psalmos,* the word translated "psalms" in Ephesians 5:19—in the phrase *"psalms, hymns, and spiritual songs."* It is defined as: "a set piece of music, i.e. a sacred ode accompanied with the voice, *harp or other instrument"* (Strong's Concordance, 5568).

The Hebrew equivalent of this word—translated "psalm" over and over in the Old Testament—is *mizmowr,* meaning: *"instrumental* music; by implication a poem set to notes" (Strong's Concordance, 4210). And, this word is linked with *zamar,* meaning: *"to touch the strings or parts of a musical instrument, i.e. play upon it;* to make music, accompanied by the voice" (Strong's Concordance, 2167).

So there you have it. Inherent in the very word "psalm"—whether in Greek or Hebrew—is the idea of *instrumental* music.

Imagine the people of a non-instrumental congregation singing Psalm 150! They would be singing about praising God in his sanctuary with all kinds of musical instruments: trumpet, harp, lyre, tambourine, strings, flute, and cymbals!

Psalm 87:3-7, anciently and in modern times, has been commonly applied to the church: "Glorious things are spoken of thee, O *city of God....*The highest himself shall establish her....Both the singers and THE PLAYERS ON INSTRUMENTS shall be there" (cf. Heb. 12:22, Rev. 21:9,10). If this passage does indeed refer to the church, the case for the use of musical instruments is unmistakable.

In Jesus' parable of the Prodigal Son, the time of celebration included instrumental *music* (Luke 15:25). The word translated "music" is *sumphonia,* "unison of sound ('symphony') i.e. a concert of *instruments"*(Strong's Concordance, 4858). If we allow that this parable can picture one who strays from God, but who repents, and ultimately returns to the Church—the Father's House— it puts instrumental music in a good light. The elder brother in the parable, on the other hand, upon approaching the father's house, "heard music...was angry, and would not go in" (Luke 15:25-28). There are some, today, who will not worship with their brethren, if they hear music in the Father's House!

When writing to Christians at Corinth, Paul mentioned the use of the flute, harp, and trumpet as an illustration (1 Cor. 14:7,8). If he believed it was wrong to use musical instruments during worship services, this would have been a good opportunity to make that point.

In the very next chapter, he spoke of the sounding of "the *trumpet* of God," when believers, living and dead, would be gathered at the Lord's coming (1 Cor. 15:52; cf. 1 Thess. 4:16,17; 2 Thess. 2:1; Matt. 24:31). If the use of musical instruments at a gathering of believers is inappropriate, how can we explain that a *trumpet*—whether literal or figurative—was linked with the greater gathering described here?

For any who suppose musical instruments are not mentioned as a part of New Testament worship, what about the book of Revelation that mentions *harps*— thousands of them?

The Four Living Creatures and the Twenty-four Elders are pictured as worshipping the Lamb, "every one of them having harps"—thus 28 harps (Rev. 5:8,9). The 144,000 redeemed from the earth, are said to play harps and sing before the throne—thus 144,000 harps (Rev. 14:1-3). Still others—victorious believers—are mentioned as "having the harps of God...and they sing" (Rev. 15:2).

In these passages, singing and harp playing are mentioned in a *worship* context, and that within the *heavenly* realm. If thousands of harps were not improper in Heaven, we fail to see that it is *un*-heavenly to use them in church. If any argue that the word "harp" in Revelation is symbolical, this does not change the basic point. If a harp was *bad,* it could not serve as a valid symbol for something *good.*

There are pastors who grew up in the non-musical Church of Christ. Here they heard the gospel, received Christ as Savior, and were baptized. Here it was they went to pray and study the Bible. Eventually they entered the ministry within this church. Here they may have parents, relatives, and friends. But in time, they realize the music issue is not as major as they were taught. Some remain within their church, minister to their congregation, but cannot in good conscience be dogmatic about their non-musical roots. I have heard of some congregations, now, that do allow a piano or some other instrument on some occasions.

It is also true that instrumental churches will sometimes purposely sing a song without any accompaniment. Singing a cappella, with parts, has a distinct quality and provides a nice reprieve. Clearly, the use of musical instruments is not essential to the worship of God. But— and this is our point—to insist that no musical instruments be used, *is not essential either.*

ONLY WORSHIP CHORUSES?

I once heard a visiting preacher say the church should throw away all the hymnbooks! He favored singing only "worship choruses." But the Bible speaks of "psalms *and* hymns *and* spiritual songs" (Eph. 5:19)—not just one type of songs.

Worship choruses—with words addressed *to God*— are fine. But singing, according to the Scriptures, should also serve to "teach and admonish *one another"* (Col. 3:16).

We have a rich heritage of great hymns written over the past centuries. I see no purpose in casting them aside, as though only new songs are valid for today's church.

It seems difficult to believe, but I heard about one church that sings *only* new songs—literally! During each week the worship team learns new choruses which are sung on the following Sunday, and not repeated. Next week the singing will consist of more new choruses! I suppose a basis for this extreme practice is sought in the scripture about singing "a new song" (Rev. 14:3).

Some churches feel it is more worshipful to *stand* while singing—for the *entire* song service, a half hour or more. Those who sit down may not be considered "as spiritual" as the others. But the physical makeup of some people, simply does not permit standing a long time. If an overhead projector is being used, those sitting, while others in front of them are standing, may not be able to see the words.

Are people more receptive to the Holy Spirit while standing? We should not forget that when the Spirit was outpoured at Pentecost, those original believers were "sitting" (Acts 2:2). I am convinced the position of the body is not nearly as important as the attitude of the *heart*.

A church that always had a song leader, may decide it is better to have a worship team. Some have neither—the piano player just starts playing and singing; the others join in. This way, it is believed, they are singing unto the Lord, not watching someone lead the song service. I know of one church that did away with the song service itself. Instead, for the first forty-five minutes everyone just praised the Lord out loud.

Within a church there may be those that like the beat and excitement of songs with a fast, hand-clapping tempo. Others draw close to the Lord with what they sense to be the more reverent depth of slower hymns. A wise pastor can bring all sides together, by pointing out that Christians are to consider one another. He can get them to agree that no one should be excluded—young or old. He can inspire them to stretch, to use these differences as an opportunity to practice scriptural unity, for the greater good. Why not include something for everyone? Only that which is unscriptural or offensive need be rejected.

NO NAME CHURCH?

While some groups have debated about the correct *name* of the church, a few have chosen not to have any name at all—at least not on the building. Some years ago, while speaking several places in Texas, I was scheduled to speak at a Saturday night service for one of these churches. It had grown to several hundred in attendance. They met in a former warehouse. Though it was located in a large city, and it would be dark when I got there, I did not foresee any problem. But, as service time drew near, I could not find the building! I phoned the pastor's house, but no one was home—they had already left for church! There was no way to look in the phone book for a church without a name. When trying to get directions, people would ask: "What is the *name* of the church?" I never did find it!

If a church uses no name, it might end up being known as the "No Name Church," like the first freeway exit east of Glenwood Springs, Colorado: "No Name Road."

The reason some don't use a name, is because they believe the church is the *people,* not the building. However, there is really nothing wrong with calling the building where Christians assemble a church. Paul seems to have used it in this sense: "When you come together in the church..." (1 Cor. 11:18, cf. verse 34). Today, by common usage, "church" can mean the *people*, the *service*, or the *building*.

This is also true of the word "synagogue." In Acts 13:42,43 we read: "And when the Jews were gone out of the *synagogue*....when the *congregation* was broken up..." The words "synagogue" and "congregation" are translated from the same Greek word, *sunagoge*, defined as "an assemblage of persons; specifically a Jewish 'synagogue,' the meeting *or the place"* (Strong's Concordance, 4864).

We know that the early Christians met in houses (Rom. 16:5; 1 Cor. 16:19; Col. 4:15). According to *Halley's*

Bible Handbook, we do not have any record of a church building (as such) prior to A.D. 222. So, there are some who preach against church *buildings!* This is a fruitless effort. *Many* who know the Lord today, came to him because they heard the gospel preached in a church building.

At a ministers' conference I attended in Houston, Texas, one of the speakers told how buildings were *talking* to him as he drove from the airport! He said government buildings talk, gas stations talk, stores talk, bars talk, houses talk, and churches talk. Of course he did not mean this in a *literal* sense. As we think about it, buildings *can* convey messages—good or bad.

As people drive past a church, they realize this is a place where people assemble to worship God. It is a place where people are taught values, honesty, and right living. It can serve as a lighthouse in a community, week after week, year after year. We would ask those who oppose church buildings: Would it be better to live in a totally secular society that allows no church buildings?

Over the centuries, some have felt they were honoring God by constructing elaborate and expensive cathedral-type buildings. God looks on the heart. But in stark contrast, I have been in a very poor section of Mexico with a pastor whose little "church" was made from tree limbs and sticks tied together, plastered with mud, and to which pieces of cardboard were attached on the inside. This was the best they could do. We can rejoice that God's blessings are not limited to those who can afford expensive buildings!

SANCTUARY STYLES

Some like the inside of a church to have a religious appearance—with pulpit, crosses, communion table, Bibles and hymn books in the pews—as a place of spiritual refreshing, a *contrast* to secular buildings. Others feel visitors are more comfortable if the church does *not* look "religious." They may replace pews with folding chairs. Still others suppose they should provide a club-like atmosphere, where people can sit around little tables and munch on snacks!

Some pastors, whose church growth required them to have multiple services, out of necessity developed a practice of sitting on a stool while they preached. To some preachers, the *stool* seemed to speak of success, so *they* started using a stool!

Some churches place the pulpit in a central position; others give the Communion table center stage. This commonly reflects a difference in emphasis—whether the service should be built around the preaching of the Word or receiving Communion.

Historic churches often had very high pulpits, requiring stairs to get up to them. Perhaps from this elevated position, before the days of microphones, sound carried better. But a high pulpit was also considered symbolic of the importance of the gospel message. Some, today, do away with the pulpit altogether and replace it with a plastic see-through podium *in front* of the platform. Some have done away with the platform itself. In some churches, what used to be a choir loft, now looks like the stage at a Rock and Roll Concert.

Over the years in the ministry, I have seen a lot of religious fads come and go.

I readily acknowledge there may be some things—even though once meaningful—that in time degenerate into mere forms. These need to be discarded. Sometimes changes are healthy; but not always. Jesus opposed *traditions* that make the word of God without effect (Matt. 15:6). But not all traditions—teachings that have been handed down, ways of doing things—are bad. Paul, writing to early Christians, said to "hold the *traditions* which you have been taught" and to "keep the *ordinances* [the same Greek word translated traditions], as I delivered them unto you" (2 Thess. 2:15; 3:6; 1 Cor. 11:2). If one goes to the extreme in opposing *all* traditions, in time this could become a tradition. Imagine a motto: "It is our tradition that we do not believe in tradition"!

CLERGY ATTIRE

In some denominations, it has long been a custom for the minister to wear a distinctive garment, especially in the pulpit. Some feel this reinforces the importance of the message and the dignity of the office. While this has never been my practice, uniforms *do* convey a message.

On the scene of an emergency, in the midst of confusion, the uniform of a policeman or security guard allows people to know who is in charge. In a court of law, the judge wears a garment reflecting his authority. The same is true with military uniforms. How creditable would an airline pilot be if he were dressed in old shabby clothes?

A personal example comes to mind. Years ago a man who attended my meetings in South Dakota, was Chief of Police for the community. In church he dressed in regular clothes, not in uniform. One day as I walked along a street, out of the corner of my eye I saw a police car pull up beside me. Stepping out of the car was the man I knew well, stopping to say hello. But now he was in *uniform!* It was an entirely different feeling, almost intimidating!

Some who oppose clergy uniforms or robes—even choir robes—cite Jesus' statement about hypocrites who went about "in long robes" (Lk. 20:46). But generally speaking, robes are spoken of in a favorable way in Scripture (Isa. 61:10, Lk. 15:22, Rev. 7:14).

Those who ministered in the Old Testament wore priestly robes (Exod. 28:4, etc.). But there is no indication this was ever a New Testament requirement. In the New Testament, *all* believers are part of a royal priesthood, each having access to God (1 Peter 2:9). For this reason, and seeking to counter the strong distinction some make between clergy and laity, in many churches a minister simply wears a suit and tie, dressing basically the same as those in the congregation.

Still others believe people can relate better to a minister who is dressed casually, so he purposely does not wear a suit and tie. Not wanting to look "religious," he will wear a sport shirt and trousers, and people are encouraged to do the same. If people have to "dress up" to come to church, they reason, there are those who simply will not come. It is more important to get them there, than to have a policy of dressing up.

On the other hand, even in secular events, people dress up for important occasions, as when a special leader is to be honored. So, some say, "Why not look our best when coming into the Lord's presence in his house?"

In Palm Springs, where we live, summers can be very hot. Some churches have a custom of coats and ties in the winter, but all of the people, including the pastor, go causal in the summer. In some tropical countries, with high humidity and no air-conditioning, to insist on a preacher wearing a coat and tie would serve no purpose. In those situations, short sleeves and, sometimes, even short pants, are not considered inappropriate.

LONG OR SHORT SERVICE?

In an age of fast food, some churches actually advertise that their services are "short." They feature, what some have termed, nice little "sermonettes" to "Christianettes." On the other hand, dragging out a service, may not be fruitful either.

I knew of a church that experienced a marvelous spiritual breakthrough—people coming to the Lord, an outpouring of love and spontaneous seeking of God. Services automatically became longer. So later, even when things were not happening in the same way, they felt that having a long service was a measure of spirituality.

I recall some people telling me about those "other churches" that let out at 12 noon, but that their service goes until 1:30! A good service is not necessarily how long or how short, but whether the Holy Spirit does his work in the lives of people.

The New Testament does not spell out details on how a worship service must be conducted. That is, it does not specify an opening prayer, three songs, prayer requests, announcements, offering, a special number, sermon, and closing song, in some certain order. But, it does teach that services are to be *orderly* (1 Cor. 14:40; Col. 2:5).

Before the Christians at Corinth understood this, their services were chaotic and disorderly. Had we visited that church, we too might have said they were "mad" or "insane" (cf. 1 Cor. 14:23). Several might be giving messages in tongues, all at the same time. For the individuals involved, it was exciting; but others—unable to understand what was being said—were not edified. There was confusion.

Paul was not "quenching the Spirit" when he gave guidelines for the proper use of spiritual gifts. He did *not* forbid them to speak in tongues (1 Thess. 5:19; 1 Cor. 14:39). He pointed out that during his own personal devotions, the Holy Spirit enabled him to pray, praise, and sing in another tongue. Yet *in the church*—the public meeting, during the service—he said he would rather speak five words in a language they could understand, than ten thousand words in a language they could not understand (1 Cor. 14:18,19).

Perhaps using the principle about the testimony of two or three witnesses (2 Cor. 13:1, Deut. 19:15), Paul said messages in tongues should be two or three—one at a time—followed by interpretation. But if no one with the gift of interpretation was present, the person giving a message in tongues should speak unto himself and to God, without interrupting the service (1 Cor. 14:27,28).

In one of my meetings years ago, a visiting pastor led a testimony service. Over in one section a woman stood to testify. When she had no sooner started, he pointed to another section and asked for someone there to stand and testify. Then, quickly, he asked someone in another section. Soon three or four at a time were testifying! It seemed *exciting*—so many testifying for the Lord at the same time. But it was difficult to understand what any of them said. Did he not know the biblical principle that people should speak one at a time, so all can understand and be edified?

LET WOMEN BE SILENT?

As Paul wrote about services being conducted in an orderly manner, he also addressed a situation involving *women* at Corinth—they were to be *silent* in the church. Failing to understand his words *in context,* some have based radical conclusions on these few words!

In the ancient world, if education was available, it was for men—seldom for women. Consequently, it was more difficult for women to understand things that were being preached. Desiring to understand, they would speak out, asking questions. This had become a distraction, causing confusion in the services. Instead of doing this, Paul said they should wait and ask their husbands at home. It was in *this* context that Paul said, "Let your women keep silence in the church" (1 Cor. 14:34-35).

If this statement is taken in an absolute sense, it would not only rule out women preaching—it would mean women could not sing, testify, pray, make announcements, or have *any* vocal part in a church service.

It is commonly overlooked that just a few verses before, Paul said in effect: "Let your *men* keep silence in the church"! If a man gave a message in another tongue, it was to be interpreted. But if no one with the gift of interpretation was present, "let *him* keep silence in the church" (verse 28)—essentially the same wording. No one takes this to mean a *man* cannot preach, sing, testify, pray, or make announcements. To be consistent, the same rule of interpretation should apply in both verses.

Did women need to ask their husbands questions at home because men are smarter than women? I suppose some might draw this erroneous conclusion. But recognizing the *educational* differences between men and women at the time, provides a better explanation. That Paul did not require the *total* silence of women is evident: earlier in the *same* book, he referred to women praying and prophesying at Corinth (1 Cor. 11:4,5; cf. Acts 2:17; 21:9).

Paul mentioned a woman named Phebe, "a servant of the church at Cenchrea" (only six miles from Corinth!), who had been of special help to him and was to be received by the saints, even at Rome (Rom. 16:1,2).

He mentioned Euodias and Syntyche, women that "labored with me in the gospel, with Clement also, and with other my fellow laborers" (Phil. 4:2,3).

He referred to Aquila and Priscilla, husband and wife, as his dedicated helpers (Rom. 16:3). They—Aquila *and* Priscilla—were effectively used of the Lord to "expound the way of God" to Apollos (Acts 18:26).

Paul regarded Andronicus and Junia (a woman) as "outstanding among the apostles" (Rom. 16:7). And, weighty are his words: "There is neither male nor female, for you are all *one* in Christ Jesus" (Gal. 3:28).

If Paul held a negative view regarding women, as some suppose, these verses would be difficult to explain!

DECENTLY AND IN ORDER

It is beneficial for a church—especially a large church—to have a good sound system. But if the sound is turned up so loud it nearly blasts people away, this too can be out of order. "God is not the author of confusion, but of peace....Let all things be done decently and in order" (1 Cor. 14:33,40).

When I was a teenager, a preacher with some big ideas came to Riverside, California, to hold a meeting. Supposing he would draw a large crowd, he rented the City Auditorium that seated 2,000 people. My mother and I went to the meeting, swelling the "crowd" to a total of 17 people! When the piano player did not show up, needing a volunteer, I went up on the stage to play the large grand piano for the song service. From this vantage point, that group of 17 people looked especially small in this large auditorium! As the preacher yelled into the microphone—with the volume obviously set on high—the sound echoing around that near-empty auditorium was LOUD.

A man, about 15 rows back, stood up, waving his hands, and said: "If you don't turn that microphone down I'm going to leave. In fact," he continued, "I think I'll leave anyhow!"

Some years ago, I spoke at a church on the east coast. As a result of invitations I sent out, a medical doctor, who had shown interest in my writings, came to the meeting. The music was so loud, he sat there holding his ears! I thought he might leave, but he was good-natured about it, enjoyed my message, and visited a while afterward.

I appreciate *enthusiasm*—the people of God should be upbeat and joyful. But should a church try to duplicate the loud, deafening sounds of a Rock Concert? Doesn't common sense indicate a balance? The volume should be loud enough to be easily heard—not so loud it gives people headaches!

Loud noise, if only for the sake of noise, misses the mark. When the Ark of the Covenant was brought from Shiloh, "all Israel shouted with a great shout, so that the earth rang again" (1 Sam. 4:5). The very wording implies this was unique—not the norm for *every* service. If we truly understand the moving of the Spirit, the greater depth may not be in the noise, but in a blessed quietness or even weeping before him. God can be in the loud; he can

63

also be in the quiet, when we are *still* before the Lord, knowing that he is God (Ps. 46:10).

In most churches a conversational tone is the norm for a preacher; in some, hollering is considered forceful. "The kind of preacher I like," one man told me, "is the kind you can hear gasping for breath two blocks down the street!"

The fact that on one occasion the Lord told Isaiah to *"cry aloud* and spare not" (Isa. 58:1), implies this was not his *normal* preaching style. If he *always* hollered, these instructions would have been unnecessary. IF I PUT THIS SENTENCE IN CAPS, OR A WORD HERE AND THERE, IT PROVIDES EMPHASIS AND DRAWS ATTENTION! But if this entire book were printed in caps, nothing would be emphasized.

LOUD AND FAST

Back in the 1950s, Pentecostal preacher, Theodore Fitch, wrote a book: *How To Be A Successful Minister.* He sought to provide words of wisdom to his fellow-preachers who, in their enthusiasm, felt they must always preach loud and fast. In so doing, they would use a lot of fill-in words like "Amen," "praise the Lord," or "glory to God." To illustrate, he made up the following story about a preacher describing a car accident:

> I saw this car, Amen, coming at a terrific pace, praise God. It was weaving, Amen, all over the road, Amen, praise the Lord. I started to pull off the road, Amen, but his car hit the back end of my car, glory to God, Amen. There was a terrible crash, praise God, Amen. My uncle, Amen, who was riding in the back seat, Amen, was killed instantly, thank God. It was a horrible ordeal, praise God.

> My mother-in-law, thank God, was also riding in the back seat, Amen, praise God. She was badly cut and bruised, Amen, thank God. We thought she would die, praise God, before we would get her to the hospital, Amen, bless God. She suffered agony for days, praise

God, and finally died, thank God, Amen. Well, glory to God! Hallelujah! It was terrible! My wife's throat was badly cut, thank God, and she could not say very much for months, praise God, Amen.

This example was exaggerated, of course—to make a point. In some cases, the habit of using fill-in words was because preachers did not take time to study and properly prepare their messages. Some *purposely* would not prepare, quoting the statement of Jesus to his disciples: "...take no thought how or what you shall speak: for it shall be given you in that same hour what you shall speak" (Matt. 10:19). But this statement, as the context shows, referred to times of persecution when they would be brought before kings and rulers.

Normally, a preacher should study, plan, and prepare, so that his message maintains focus, the points are connected, and it is easy for the audience to follow. Proper preparation does not bypass the fact it still takes the Holy Spirit to make the message truly effective.

As a man was leaving a certain church, he told the pastor there were *three* things he did not like about his sermon. "First of all," he said, "you *read* your sermon. Second, you are *not* a good reader. And third, *I didn't like what you read!*"

Sermons and services that are too predictable, too routine, too structured, miss the mark. But this does not justify going to the other extreme of turning a service into a free-for-all. On the spur of the moment someone may be called "to lead some songs." The pianist is not prepared, not knowing which songs will be sung. But they make it through a song service.

When prayer requests are taken, unless there is balance, it can be discouraging—taking too long to hear details about all the ones that are sick, facing operations, about to go bankrupt, or having trouble with their sons and daughters.

After prayer, someone calls out, "I'd like to hear Sister Sally sing a special!" But Sister Sally says she can't, she has a cold. "Well, how about Brother Bob—can he do one for us?" Bob comes up, asking for prayer—says he has not practiced. Things have not been going well for him. "The Devil has been after me all week," he says. Someone else chimes in, "Good! If he's still 'after' you, he hasn't caught you yet!"

This reminds me of a church, a pioneer work, where I preached once when I was about 20 years old. Following the hit-and-miss preliminaries, I was about five minutes into my message. The pastor (who was seated behind me on the platform) jumped up, patted me on the back, and pointing toward the people, said: "That's real good preach'n, brother! What else are ya gonna tell 'em?" Every few minutes he would do this, amid a lot of "Amens" and "Praise the Lords" from the congregation. Had videos been available then, that would be something to see! We could probably all have a few good laughs of me preaching and that man jumping up, patting me on the back, pointing toward the people and saying: "That's real good preach'n, brother! What else are ya gonna tell 'em?"

None of this is intended in a critical way. I acknowledge that people have come to Christ in all kinds of services. I also know that God looks on the heart. But *ideally,* while avoiding the extreme of cold formalism, we should not go to the extreme of wild fanaticism.

Years ago I knew a young man who grew up in a church that liked wild services. When he was in his 20s, he became the pastor of this church. For structural stability, the building had horizontal, pipe-like crossbars that extended from wall to wall beneath an open-beam ceiling.

One night while preaching, he ran and jumped up on top of the pulpit. With a gigantic leap, he grabbed one of those crossbars and swung clear up and over like a circus trapeze performer—never missing a word! They *really* "had church" that night! He had a lot of enthusiasm and this was his way of showing it. But most Christians would be turned off by such gymnastics.

If actions are *perceived* as lacking reverence—even though not intended that way—they can short-circuit and discredit whatever truth is being preached. It has been said that God has chosen to save people "by the foolishness of preaching"—not by foolish preaching (cf. 1 Cor. 1:21).

Using the scripture that God will "bruise Satan under your feet" (Rom. 16:20), a Los Angeles preacher would tell the people in his church to stomp on the Devil. For a while, it became a regular part of each service. They would literally jump up and down, stomping the floor as though the Devil was under their feet!

PILLOW POUNDING SERVICE

Some years ago, a man I was visiting in Oakland, California, wanted me to go with him to hear a preacher who was holding some special meetings. A unique feature of these meetings was "Pillow Pounding." The purpose of using a pillow, I learned, was to bring sins or frustrations out into the open. A woman having trouble with her husband would pretend the pillow was her husband and, in the name of the Lord, begin pounding it (him). Or a person might pretend the pillow was Satan. Whatever one might want to tell Satan, he would tell the pillow. In beating up the pillow, he would, supposedly, be beating up Satan!

It ended up there was no pillow pounding in the afternoon service we attended. But I talked to a woman there who told me about a service in which hundreds of people were pounding pillows. She said that when some of the pillows broke open—and feathers were floating around in the air—it "looked like an appearance of the Shekinah glory"!

I am reminded, just now, of an incident that occurred during a large three-day meeting in Las Vegas, Nevada, at which I was one of the speakers. Someone else set up the meeting; so I had nothing to do with the preliminaries. On the closing night, as I arrived, I noticed the end of a fairly large plastic pipe extending from beneath the platform. I asked the man in charge, "What is this?" He smiled and said I would soon understand.

When the time came, as several women dressed in white moved about in worshipful dance steps, a cloud of fog began coming from the pipe. (I believe this was accomplished by using dry ice.) Beneath bright lights, others in procession carried banners with glittering words like "Jehovah Jirah" or "Jesus is Lord," intermingling with the dancers, in a dynamic production within this cloud-like appearance.

It was not a supernatural cloud—no one pretended it was. But, if one could look beyond the somewhat artificial nature of the whole thing, it did bring to mind those times when God did send a cloud of his glory (Exod. 40:34; 1 Kings 8:10,11; Matt. 17:5).

PUBLIC CONFESSION MEETINGS

Some churches have public confession meetings, encouraging people to confess their weaknesses, temptations, and secret thoughts. The intended purpose is to bring such things out into the open and purge away guilt. At the time of Nehemiah, during a time of national repentance, people "stood and confessed their sins, and the iniquities of their fathers" (Neh. 9:2). But balance is needed, for this is a vulnerable area!

I know a pastor's wife who publicly confessed in one of these meetings that she "never liked her mother-in-law." Like her or not, that woman was the pastor's mother, the grandmother of their children, and a member of the church! Such confession did not bring cleansing—it brought confusion! Since only *God* knew about this wrong attitude, she should have confessed to *him!*

As a result of receiving Christ as Savior, an unmarried couple with several children wanted to be legally married. To do so, they were told their past sins and mistakes must be made *public*. God does not require this. We have all sinned and come short of the glory of God. As sinners we come to Christ for salvation. He saves us from our sins. We can testify about this, but it is not necessary to explain all the details! We are now new creatures in Christ, we have "no fellowship with the unfruitful works of darkness"; it is "a shame to speak of those things which are done in secret" (Eph. 5:11,12).

The wife of a pastor (who was away on a missionary trip) made a mistake and fell into immorality in a one-time incident. Feeling tremendous remorse for her actions, she confided in a woman she considered deeply spiritual. The woman said she could not be right with God unless she confessed to her husband, to the other man's wife, and made a public confession to the church!

When she told her husband, he turned against her and later used it as grounds for divorce. When she confessed to the other man's wife, she was deeply hurt and would not forgive her. The man she had been involved with also turned against her. When she confessed to the church, several families left the church. Some believe, and not without good reasons, she would have been better to confess to God and be less public with people.

While the Bible does say, "Confess your faults one to another, and pray one for another" (James 5:16), it should be carefully noted it says "your" faults, not the faults or sins of someone else. In the incident of the pastor's wife, in confessing her sin, she automatically confessed the sin of *someone else!*

Even in giving public prayer requests, caution is in order. I recall when I was a teenager, our pastor asked prayer for a man who attended the church, but was not present at this particular mid-week prayer meeting: "Let's pray for [calling him by name]—someone in his neighbor-hood got out a story about him being a 'peeping Tom'." I am sure, even long after this, some may have wondered if the "story" was true!

SITUATION ETHICS?

A teaching, sometimes called "Situation Ethics," claims that the right or wrong of anything depends on the situation. Suppose a crazed murderer has just escaped from prison, comes to our door with a gun in his hand, intending to kill an innocent person who is staying with us. Are we obligated to tell him that person is there? In that situation, wouldn't it be better to make up a story, head him in a different direction, and protect the inno-cent? Of course. But, be assured, this would be an ex-ceptional case and a very unlikely one at that! To cite *exceptions* like this, calling it situation ethics, and make it a rule, can hardly be justified.

But, in balance, situations can alter cases. "Have you not read what David did when he was hungry...how he entered into the house of God, and did eat the shewbread, which was not lawful for him to eat...but only for the priests?" (Matt. 12:3,4; 1 Sam. 21:6).

Jesus asked the Twelve: "When I sent you without purse, and script, and shoes, lacked you anything?"—referring back to Matthew 10:9,10. And they said, "Noth-ing." Then said he unto them, "But *now*, he that has a purse let him take it, and likewise his scrip: and he that has no sword, let him sell his garment, and buy one" (Luke 22:35-38).

Some things that may be required "for the present distress" (1 Cor. 7:26), to use Paul's words, may not apply under different circumstances.

God's word to Noah was to build an ark. That is over and past. Yet the *principle* remains: Christ becomes our Ark of Safety through the storms of life. Not everything in the Bible applies in the same way. Covetousness is wrong, of course. But the Tenth Commandment would not apply in the letter of the law—most people are not tempted to covet a neighbor's donkey (Exod. 20:17). Most neighbors don't own donkeys! Today, with paved streets and travel by automobile, we would not *literally* "shake off the dust of our feet" (Matt. 10:14).

An American missionary asked a native why his people put food on a grave—obviously a dead man cannot *eat*. His reply was a question: "Why do Americans put flowers on a grave—can a dead man *smell?*" A missionary's job is to preach the gospel, not to "Americanize" people of another country. They have a right to their national heritage, history, culture, and ways of doing things—unless, of course, those things have an idolatrous or demonic linkage.

The fact that some customs are mentioned in the Bible, does not necessarily mean *we* must adopt them in our culture. For example, back then, if a man's married brother died without children, he would marry the widow. But if he refused, "then shall his brother's wife come unto him in the presence of the elders, and loose his shoe from off his foot, and spit in his face" (Deut. 25:5-10). Does anyone suppose this custom applies today? Customs and commandments are in two separate categories.

When Paul wrote, "Greet one another with a holy kiss" (1 Cor. 16:20; 1 Thess. 5:26), a kiss was a generally accepted custom at that time and place. Today, the *principle* remains—Christians are to be friendly and greet one another—but the *equivalent* greeting in this country, and many others, is a warm handshake.

Those who try to follow the letter-of-the-law, supposing Christians *must* literally greet one another with a kiss, face unnecessary problems. Picture a pastor who stands at the door greeting people as they leave church. One couple approaches—the wife is a Christian, the husband does not profess to be a Christian. If the pastor kisses the wife, this may not set well with her husband! If he greets the man with a kiss, he may never come back! If he greets the "saved" with a kiss, and the "unsaved" with a handshake, he has become judge and jury.

There is a certain warmth in greeting fellow Christians as "brother" and "sister"—it has a biblical basis and we are certainly not against it. But, again, wisdom is in order. Suppose we are greeting various ones from the pulpit. If we refer to one man as "Brother" and another as "Mr.," it immediately appears we consider one to be a true Christian. The other one, we are not sure about!

It can work the other way also. I had some relatives that visited a church and filled out a visitors' card. They were welcomed from the pulpit with these words: "We are glad to have *Brother and Sister* _____ with us today." They were not Christians, so did not appreciate the titles! For these reasons, some prefer using actual names, rather than adding titles.

There are some who think a woman should not use the title Ms.—that it should be either Miss or Mrs. But the title Mr. does not reveal whether a man is married or not. Why should a woman be required to reveal *her* marital status? Someone has written:

When you call me Miss or Mrs.
   You invade my private life,
For it's not the public's business
   If I am, or was, a wife.

A pastor once told me about a man who visited his service. Seeking some special recognition, it would seem, he had an usher take his business card up to the pulpit. On it, he claimed he was a "Prophet"—a *"major* Prophet, *not* a minor Prophet"!

Before speaking at a church near Dallas, Texas, some years ago, the pastor told me: "Occasionally we have a man come to our service who thinks he is Jesus Christ— he may be here today." Sure enough, just as the service

72

was turned to me, toward the back of the building a man stood: "I am the resurrection and the life," he proclaimed, "he that believeth in me shall not perish, but have everlasting life. I am the Light of the world. Yea, I am Jesus Christ, the Savior." He said a few more things, pointing out that he had come to the meeting—"not to be ministered to, but to minister"—and, having said this, *left!*

We are all familiar with the practice of asking people who want to accept Christ to "come forward." I know a pastor that does it a different way: instead of having them come *forward,* he invites them to go to the *back* of the church where personal workers will talk and pray with them. This method discourages anyone from walking out during the Invitation!

In welcoming visitors to a service, there are churches that ask them to stand and give their names. But another method some use is less intimidating. They have everyone else stand—*except* the visitors—while those close by shake their hands and welcome them.

A preacher I met a few years ago mentioned his brother-in-law, who was also in the ministry. Because they were in different denominations, with some conflicting beliefs, their relationship had been strained for years. But, the last time I saw him, he said things had improved. He had gone to see his brother-in-law, who told him as he was leaving: "If you are in our area again, and come to church, I would like to have you lead in *silent* prayer"!

PEOPLE INVOLVEMENT

Services in some churches feature those on the stage as performers; the others are simply spectators. But in the early church, audience participation was encouraged. Everyone could take part, providing the church was edified (1 Cor. 14:26). As churches grew larger, the *principle* of people involvement remained, but everyone in every service could not take part, for obvious reasons.

Some years ago at a Bible conference in San Diego, California, I was scheduled to be the night speaker. As I recall, 109 preachers were given an opportunity to introduce themselves, tell where they were from, and a little about their ministries. They were not supposed to "preach," but many of them did! After three hours and this many speakers, the service was turned to me for the evening message!

A few churches believe in what they call "open pulpit." The idea is that *anyone*, not just the pastor, can come to the pulpit and speak. This way, it is believed, a group is not subjected to the controlled censorship of some ecclesiastical hierarchy. If the Lord has revealed anything to anyone, he is free to share it from the pulpit. A service may have several speakers. The downside, based on what I have observed, is that there is no clear message.

One speaker may preach in favor of eternal security, another against eternal security. One may preach against eating pork. Another may be against candy bars and coffee. Right or wrong, some will make their point; others only ramble. A mature Christian might be able to sort all this out, but for new converts and young people, it can be confusing and detrimental.

Back around 1970 I knew some people who belonged to a fellowship of churches that promoted the "open pulpit" concept. They sincerely hungered for truth. They would all get together several times a year for what they called "Threshing Floor" meetings. Driving day and night to get there, busloads would gather from various parts of the country. Anyone in the group could bring up any Bible-related subject for discussion and debate.

Differences might range from those who did not believe there is a personal Devil (that evil is really only our flesh), to those who believed most people, including believers, need deliverance from demons! Sessions, conducted in an orderly manner, would run for six hours. By doing this, they believed they would ultimately all see "eye to eye" (Isa. 52:8). But, the last I heard, they were *more divided than ever!*

As a young preacher, I knew a wonderful woman who regarded me like one of her family. Years later, as had been her request, I conducted her funeral. She loved God, and wanted to know the Bible truth about *everything.* In the process, she was pulled many directions. She received stacks of literature from a variety of churches and ministries. But all the conflicting doctrines she encountered, instead of bringing peace, tended to rob her of peace!

How should we explain the book of Revelation? Where is the United States in Bible prophecy? Are the Jews God's chosen people? How should we explain the Trinity? Should we vote and salute the flag? What about blood transfusions or eating pork? Will the saved go to Heaven, or live forever on a new earth? How should one be baptized? How should we pronounce the Sacred Name? Which translation of the Bible is right?

Are the gifts of the Spirit, like speaking in tongues and healing, for us today? Which church is the one true church? Should Christians meet for worship on Sunday or Saturday? Should Christians observe the Jewish feast days? What about Easter, Christmas, and birthday celebrations—are they pagan?

And the time would fail me to tell of the rapture, tribulation, millennium, three days and nights, Jewish calendar, the state of the dead, Hell, spirits in prison, the curse on Ham, sons of God looking on daughters of men, a pre-Adamic earth, seed of the serpent, age of the earth, dinosaurs, fossils, etc., etc.!

There is nothing wrong with studying any of these things, but one must maintain balance. Trying to figure out "everything" about "everything" is not realistic. Food is good, but all kinds of food—or too much at a time—can cause indigestion! (cf. Heb. 5:11-14).

BIBLE CONTRADICTIONS?

In my younger years, I preached there were no contradictions in the Bible—I didn't think there were. But as time went on, I did notice some things that had the *appearance*, at least, of being contradictory.

In 1973, having access to a mountain cabin, I set aside some days to go there for prayer and soul searching. While reading through the writings of Ezra and Nehemiah, I noticed that each records a detailed list of the various family groups that returned from the Babylonian captivity, giving names and numbers. Each list ends with the words: "The whole congregation together was 42,360" (Ezra 2:64; Neh. 7:66). Here, then, was an opportunity to compare information.

The family of Parosh is mentioned first on each list. The book of Ezra says they numbered 2,172 people; Nehemiah says the same: 2,172. Next were those of the family of Shephatiah. Ezra says they numbered 372; Nehemiah says they numbered 372. Next were those of the family of Arah. Ezra says they numbered 775; *but Nehemiah says they numbered 652!*

It was obvious: these numbers did *not* match. I wondered: What about the rest of the numbers on these two lists? I took a piece of paper, drew two columns, and carefully listed the names and numbers. This information is reproduced in the accompanying table. The numbers in bold type, it will be noticed, do not agree with each other.

Both Ezra and Nehemiah give 42,360 as the total. But if we add up the numbers on Ezra's list, the total is 29,818. If we add up the numbers on Nehemiah's list, the total is 31,089. The two lists do not agree with each other, and neither list agrees with itself!

Were Ezra and Nehemiah liars? Did they misrepresent facts? Of course not. What would be their motive? There is no reason to doubt that each list, when written, was accurate. But as these handwritten records were

EZRA 2:3—64.		NEHEMIAH 7:8—66.	
Parosh	2,172	Parosh	2,172
Shephatiah	372	Shephatiah	372
Arah	**775**	**Arah**	**652**
Pahath-moab	**2,812**	**Pahath-moab**	**2,818**
Elam	1,254	Elam	1,254
Zattu	**945**	**Zattu**	**845**
Zaccai	760	Zaccai	760
Bani	**642**	**Binnui**	**648**
Bebai	**623**	**Bebai**	**628**
Azgad	**1,222**	**Azgad**	**2,322**
Adonikam	**666**	**Adonikam**	**667**
Bigvai	**2,056**	**Bigvai**	**2,067**
Adin	**454**	**Adin**	**655**
Ater	98	Ater	98
Bezai	**323**	**Bezai**	**324**
Jorah	112	Hariph	112
Hashum	**223**	**Hashum**	**328**
Gibbar	95	Gibeon	95
Bethlehem	**123**	**Bethlehem and**	
Netophah	**56**	**Netophah (combined)**	**188**
Anathoth	128	Anathoth	128
Azmaveth	42	Beth-azmaveth	42
Kerjatharim, Chephirah, and		Kirjathjearim, Chephirah,	
Beeroth	743	and Beeroth	743
Ramah and Gaba	621	Ramah and Gaba	621
Michmas	122	Michmas	122
Bethel and Ai	**223**	**Bethel and Ai**	**123**
Nebo	52	Nebo	52
Magbish	**156**	**[omitted]**	
Elam (other)	1,254	Elam (other)	1,254
Harim	320	Harim	320
Jerico	345	Jerico	345
Lod, Hadid, Ono	**725**	**Lod, Hadid, Ono**	**721**
Senaah	**3,630**	**Senaah**	**3,930**
Jedaiah of Jeshua	973	Jedaiah of Jeshua	973
Immer	1,052	Immer	1,052
Pashur	1,247	Pashur	1,247
Harim	1,017	Harim	1,017
Jeshua, Hodaviah	74	Jeshua, Hodaviah	74
Asaph	**128**	**Asaph**	**148**
Shallum, Ater, Talmon, Akkub,		**Shallum, Ater, Talmon, Akkub,**	
Hatita, Shobai	**139**	**Hatita, Shobai**	**138**
List of Nethinims and children of		List of Nethinims and children of	
Solomon's servants	392	Solomon's servants	392
Some without pedigree	**652**	**Some without pedigree**	**642**
Total	**29,818**	**Total**	**31,089**

"The whole congregation together was 42,360" (Ezra 2:64)

"The whole congregation together was 42,360" (Neh. 7:66).

copied and re-copied, once a mistake was made, the next copyist repeated it, honestly copying what was in front of him. Considering the primitive quality of ancient writing materials, poor lighting, no eyeglasses, and other factors, it is understandable how numbers could be confused.

By the time the King James Version, The New American Standard, The New International Version, or any other English version of the Bible, was translated, the differences were already there.

Pointing out that *numbers* in ancient manuscripts are especially vulnerable, esteemed biblical commentator Adam Clarke (1760 - 1832), cites a verse that says David slew the men of seven *hundred* chariots. The parallel verse says it was seven *thousand* chariots (2 Sam. 10:18; 1Chron. 19:18). He goes on to show how the Hebrew letter used to designate seven *hundred* is very similar to the one used to designate seven *thousand*. This close similarity could easily cause a copiest to mistake one for the other. Even in English, especially when handwritten, a 1 might look like an l, a 5 might look like an S, a 9 might look like a 4, etc.

We live in an imperfect world. Cars are not *perfect,* still they can take us where we need to go. A job is not *perfect,* yet it provides a paycheck. A local church is not *perfect,* yet it can be used of God. One can be saved through the preaching of the gospel, even though the preacher is not *perfect.* If ancient copyists made mistakes here and there as they copied numbers—if their work was not *perfect*—this is no reason to throw the Bible away.

Does it really matter whether the family of Arah numbered 775—or 652? Is it important whether David's enemies had 700—or 7,000—chariots? Sometimes people get hung up on technical points *about* the Bible, and fail to grasp the overall message of the Bible itself. Perhaps there is a greater lesson in all of this: that we do not become too dogmatic, knowing that the letter kills, but the spirit gives life (2 Cor. 3:6).

I have always been a *Bible* preacher (cf. Acts 2:16; 2 Tim. 4:2, etc.). In this book nearly *400 Bible verses* are quoted or referred to. But, having said this, I must tell you: Our God is greater than any book, including the Bible. We worship *God*—not a book *about* God.

Men like Noah and Abraham knew God—before the Bible was written. Even the early Christians did not have the privilege of owning Bibles—at least not personal copies, as we have them today. Prior to the invention of the printing press, Bibles had to be copied by hand. It is figured that an industrious scribe would need a *year* to do this. How many of us could afford a year's wages in order to own a Bible?

Today we not only have Bibles, we have Bible concordances, Bible commentaries, Bible dictionaries, Bible lexicons, Bible tapes, Bible videos, Bible computer programs—all kinds of Bible-related tools. Rightly used, these things can be a helpful. But—without any of these —consider the impact made by the early Christians as they preached the simple gospel message in the power of the Holy Spirit. Even their enemies said they had "turned the world upside down"! (Acts 17:6). Multitudes received the good news, while others rejected it, sometimes with wild *fanaticism*—"crying out, casting off their clothes, and throwing dust in the air"! (Acts 22:22,23).

MAJORING ON MINORS

Back in 1962, while holding meetings in Modesto, California, I had gone to the church one morning to pray. Determined not to be distracted, when a knock came on a side door, I ignored it. (I had reason to believe it did not involve me.) But the knocking persisted, so after quite a while I finally went to the door. Here was a man who had been attending my meetings, rejoicing and crying at the same time. He told me he had hardly slept all night, that the Lord had laid something on his heart. Having just come from the bank, he handed me $800 in fifty-dollar bills, supplying a distinct financial need at the time. He was a sweet man—I know he loved God. But because of a certain belief he held, he would seldom go with his family to church.

Because the Bible speaks of names being "written in *Heaven*"(Lk. 10:20), he believed it was wrong for a church to have a membership roll. (Some who believe this way, even say that placing one's name on a church roll *removes* it from the Book of Life!) His wife and family attended church regularly, but not him—not a church that had a membership roll! Had he been able to balance this out, he would have seen that attending church was more important than his comparatively minor point.

Even though the Bible says not to forsake the assembling of ourselves together (Heb. 10:25), there are some who suppose God does not want *them* to attend church. They may quote Second Corinthians 6:17: "Come out from among them, and be separate"; or Revelation 3:20—about Jesus standing *outside* the Laodicean church, knocking on the door. *So,* if a person wants to be with *him,* they reason, he must get out of the church! Some twist the Scriptures to their own destruction (2 Peter 3:16).

Granted, a local church is not perfect and we may not agree on everything. But wouldn't it be better to cast our vote for the church (by attendance), than staying home with a critical attitude?

MISUNDERSTOOD WORDS

In 1978, I was a speaker at Glen Eyrie, the beautiful Navigators' Conference grounds, in Colorado Springs, Colorado. One afternoon I hiked up the trail to the hilltop burial site of Dawson Trotman, founder of The Navigators, who died to save the life of a drowning girl.

On the way up, I passed the wife of one of the other speakers, who was coming down the trail. She told me, "When you get up there, you can see the planes"—at least that's what I *thought* she said. I knew the large Air Force Academy was not far away. From the hilltop, I assumed, I would see many planes parked along the landing strip. But upon reaching the top, I saw no *planes*. I did notice the *plains*—extending eastward as far as the eye could see. It then dawned on me—she was talking about plains, not planes! We laughed about this later, realizing how words can be misunderstood.

When we read in Reformation history about "The Diet of Worms," it sounds like people ate worms! But "Diet" was a word used for a legislative assembly. It was before such an assembly in Worms, a city in Germany, that Martin Luther was called to make his defense in 1521.

The Pope may issue an official "Bull," which to English ears sounds strange. But when we realize that "bull," in this case, is but a shortened form of "bulletin" (a word we are more familiar with), it is no longer strange. A bulletin may be good or bad, depending on its message.

As a boy, I went to Sunday School. A friend of mine, who was Catholic, went to Catechism. "Catechism"? I knew this word didn't have anything to do with a *cat,* but had no idea what it meant. Years later, I would learn it is based on a Greek word in the Bible—*katecheo*—translated "teach" or "instruct" (1 Cor. 14:19, Lk. 1:4). If one goes to Catechism, it simply means he is going for instruction. The question would be whether this instruction is valid; the word itself is not wrong.

What is often referred to as the Lord's Supper in some churches, in others is called the "Eucharist." Some, unaccustomed to this word, may think it sounds strange, even "pagan"!

But, to the contrary, it is derived from a Greek word in the New Testament, *eucharisteo*, meaning *to be grateful.* It is used in Matthew 26:27 when Jesus took the cup and "gave thanks." If some hold erroneous views about the Eucharist, the error is not the word itself.

We would not normally use the word "angel" to describe the office of a pastor. We usually think of angels as *heavenly* messengers. But the *same* Greek word, *aggelos,* is also used of *earthly* messengers (James 2:25; Lk. 7:24). The pastors of the seven churches in Revelation are called angels: "Unto the angel of the church of Ephesus.... unto the angel of the church in Smyrna...", etc. (Rev. 2-3).

Though it commonly goes unnoticed, the word angel is the basis of our word Evangelist: Ev ANGEL ist (cf. Acts 21:8; 2 Tim. 4:5). This is true in Greek, as well as English.

Those of us who do not have an Episcopalian background may question why a minister of that denomination is called a "Rector." But once we realize this is simply a shortened form of "Director," it becomes understandable.

Terms that may be used by one denomination, may not be as common in another. Some use the term "Gospel Meeting," some "Seminar," others "Evangelistic Crusade," and still others "Revival." While it is true we don't read in the Bible about Peter or Paul going to a city to hold a "Revival," the term is not inappropriate. The Greek word for revival, *anazao,* means: "to live again" (Lk. 15:24, 32; cf. Hab. 3:2).

If any suppose we should only use words that are in the Bible, we should keep in mind the word "Bible" is not in the Bible!

Even within the Bible, word usage varied over time: "He that is now called a Prophet was beforetime called a Seer" (1 Sam. 9:9); the month that was called Abib, was later called Nisan (Deut. 16:1; Esther 3:7); what was earlier called The Feast of Weeks, was later called Pentecost (Exod. 34:22; Acts 2:1); etc.

Unless a difference in wording is of some major consequence, there is no need to "strive about words" (2 Tim. 2:14).

CORRECT NAME FOR CHURCH?

What is the correct, biblical name for the church? "The churches of Christ" is certainly a scriptural name (Rom. 16:16). It is used one time in Scripture; but the name "Church of God" is used *twelve* times. Some believe *twelve* gives this name special apostolic status.

In one town a church used the name "Church of God." A few blocks down the street, another used the name *"The* Church of God," and still another, "The *First* Church of God." In Fresno, California, one group threatened a lawsuit over who had the legal right to use the name Church of God!

Those that use the name "Church of God" commonly add extra words for clarification:

Church of God (Anderson, Indiana), Church of God (Cleveland, Tennessee), Church of God (Seventh Day), Church of God of Prophecy, Pentecostal Church of God of America, Church of God in Christ, Church of God International, The (Original) Church of God, Church of God and Saints of Christ, Remnant Church of God, Apostolic Church of God, Justified Church of God, Glorified Church of God, Holiness Church of God, Bible Church of God, Radio Church of God, Worldwide Church of God, etc.

Actually, believers who make up the church, the body of Christ, are mentioned by *many* different terms in Scripture. They are called:

The Church of God, Church of the Living God, House of God, Habitation of God, Household of God, Temple of God, Children of God, Sons of God, Family of God, Elect of God, Called of God, Flock of God, Beloved of God, Followers of God, Heirs of God, Ministers of God, and God's heritage.

They are called:

The Churches of Christ, the Body of Christ, Babes in Christ, Members of Christ, Ambassadors of Christ, Epistles of Christ, Joint Heirs with Christ, Church of the Firstborn, a Glorious Church, the Household of Faith, and the Kingdom of God's Dear Son.

They are called:

Sheep, Lambs, Vessels of Mercy, Salt of the Earth, Lively Stones, Branches, Firstfruits, Soldiers, Fishers of men, Nazarenes, Christians, Saints, Believers, Disciples, the Faithful, Kings, Priests, a Royal Priesthood, a Holy Nation, Worshippers, Workers, a Chosen Generation, One New Man, a Perfect Man, Friends, Witnesses, Bride, People of the Way, Holy Brethren, and Brethren.

Of all these terms, the most common is "brethren," with over 200 New Testament references. Sometimes the word is used of literal kin, but often of the body of believers (1 John 3:13; Heb. 2:11; etc.). If *frequency* in Scripture were to determine the correct name, "brethren" would win out!

The names of some denominations actually started as nicknames, like the METHODIST CHURCH. John and Charles Wesley, along with a small group of students at Oxford University, mutually agreed upon regular habits of Bible study, fasting, and devotions, as well as visitation to the sick, the poor, and prisoners. Because they *methodically* committed themselves to these practices, some derisively called them "Methodists." Eventually the term stuck. Though it is not found in Scripture, those practices for which the Wesleys stood are certainly scriptural.

The name CHURCH OF THE NAZARENE derives from the fact that Jesus, being from Nazareth, was called a Nazarene (Matt. 2:23; Acts 4:10). Some nicknamed the early believers in Christ as "the sect of the Nazarenes" (Acts 24:5).

The word CHRISTIAN appears to have initially been a nickname. "The disciples were called Christians *first* in Antioch" (Acts 11:26). As time went on, the term became widely used, so that even Agrippa would say to Paul: "Almost you persuade me to be a Christian" (Acts 26:28; cf. 1 Peter 4:16). If we understand "Christian" to mean one who is like Christ, this is a good word.

Because of the impact of Martin Luther's ministry on the Reformation, some came to be called LUTHERANS. However, Luther himself reportedly said they should not call themselves Lutherans, after him "a mere bag of dust," but rather Christians.

Though the word CATHOLIC is commonly linked with the ROMAN CATHOLIC Church, the word itself— an ancient designation—simply means *universal*. In the sense that the gospel is to be preached into all the world and to all people, any missionary-minded church might be called "catholic."

Some church names derive from a doctrinal emphasis. The name BAPTIST obviously has linkage with water baptism. The organization known as JEHOVAH'S WITNESSES, uses this name because of their emphasis on witnessing. The name ADVENTIST is linked with the *Advent* of Christ, more commonly referred to today as his Second Coming.

The name ASSEMBLY OF GOD is equivalent to Church of God. The Greek word translated "church" is also translated "assembly." The word itself can mean either a religious *or* a secular assembly (see Acts 19: 32,39,41). It is not exclusively a New Testament word; it is also used in reference to the Old Testament "church [assembly] in the wilderness" (Acts 7:38; cf. Heb. 2:12).

The word FOURSQUARE—though not directly used in Scripture as a church name—is linked with the Bride, the City of God (Rev. 21:16). By usage, the term has come to designate the full gospel, with no corners being cut.

If the word PENTECOSTAL were used in its literal sense, it would simply mean *fifty*—Pentecost comes fifty days after Passover. But because the outpouring of the Holy Spirit occurred on this day, Pentecost acquired a new and greater significance. Using the term "Pentecostal" generally means a belief that spiritual gifts, like speaking in tongues, are still available for the church today.

Over the past few decades the word CHARISMATIC has come into wide use. While not found in English Bibles, as such, it is based on the Greek, *charisma*. It is the word translated "gifts," referring to the gifts of the Holy Spirit (1 Cor. 12:4).

The names EPISCOPAL and PRESBYTERIAN—somewhat strange words to many English-speaking people— also derive from New Testament Greek: *episkopos*, translated "bishops" (Titus 1:7) and *presbuteros,* translated "elders" or "presbytery" (1 Tim. 4:14). The two terms, as used today, distinguish between two forms of church government. The CONGREGATIONAL Church, in contrast, favors a congregational form of government.

To sum up: Believers in Jesus Christ have been known by different names, historically, and in the Scriptures. In view of this, we should inquire of believers, regardless of which name they use: Are they doing God's work? Are they preaching the gospel? Are they winning souls? Are they reaching out to the poor? Do they love one another? Is the fruit of the Holy Spirit evident in their lives? These things, we believe, are more important than what "tag" they wear.

All Christian denominations hold certain basic beliefs in common. They believe in God. Man rebelled against God and sin entered in. Jesus, who was supernaturally conceived, lived a sinless life, and died for our sins. He was buried, but rose from the dead, ascended into Heaven, and sent back the Holy Spirit. Through him we can have eternal life. Differences? Certainly. But, compared to an unbelieving, secular world, all Christians share a whole realm of truth in common.

We lose balance if we tend to magnify only the *differences*. What message does it send? If we are right on some doctrinal point, and others are wrong, this is *all the more reason* we should not build walls. We should keep the lines of communication open. The seeds of truth may need time to grow. Paul was certainly no worldly compromiser, yet he was willing to become all things to all people, for the greater good (1 Cor. 9:20-22).

In his book *Pendulum Extremes* (pp. 206,207), David Wasmundt has written:

> If you are drowning in the ocean, you don't care what size, shape or color the lifeboat may be. It is a fact that millions of souls are drowning in the ocean called sin. They are perishing while lifeguard believers stand on shore arguing about what color to paint the lifeboat. Still other rescuers are contending over proper launching procedures. I say it's time to stop the quarreling and launch those salvation lifeboats any way we can! The church is weary of those who dogmatically insist that they alone understand all theological mysteries and therefore they alone are qualified to launch the boat.

Radicals, though they may be sincerely convinced of their dogmatism, commonly have "the feeling that everyone else is wrong except those in their own little group" (Gal. 5:20, *Living Bible* paraphrase). With a stubborn indifference, they may say, "Bless God, I am going to take my stand for truth—I don't care who doesn't like it!" Being firm in the faith is one thing, but an arrogant, divisive attitude can do great harm. Their efforts to root out weeds, may destroy the wheat also (Matt. 13:29).

The question has sometimes been asked: Is the point important enough to split the baby? (cf. 1 Kings 3:24-27).

A wise pastor can stand for what he believes, without causing unnecessary division. He might say, "I believe in Bible prophecy [or some other subject] a certain way. But I also realize that some of our people believe a different way. I do not think any less of them; we are *family!* We are family because we have the same Father—not because we all see everything exactly the same. What *I* say is not the final word. We are all learning, sorting things out. All who know Jesus as Lord are welcome in this church. We will love you and not put you down."

We are not saying it does not matter what we believe. *It does matter.* We should "prove all things, and hold fast that which is good" (1 Thess. 5:21). We should study things out—sincerely, honestly, and prayerfully. As we come to understand truth, we should hold to that truth, and firmly so. But, at the same time, keeping in mind that we don't "know it all." No one has everything figured out—nor do we need to—realizing it is more important *whom* we know, than *what* we know.

There is no need to make a "god" out of a denomination; but neither should we make a "god" out of *not* being a denomination. There is nothing wrong with a group having a distinctive history, founder, revival, or unique beginning—except when these things breed sectarianism or exclusivism. I have gleaned, directly and indirectly, from a number of different ministries, churches, and denominations over the years. I will not say, "I have no need of you!" (cf. 1 Cor. 12:21).

No one denomination or group is perfect, nor can any rightly claim to have *all* the truth. Some that are strong in one area, may be weak in another. Some that are seemingly small and insignificant, may be sharing a neglected truth that others overlook or avoid.

Some that are not too deep, theologically speaking, may be good at reaching new converts with the simple gospel message. Others may be so theologically deep, they miss the flow of the Holy Spirit. The ideal balance is to worship God "in spirit *and* in truth, for the Father seeks such to worship him" (John 4:23).

In his book *Approaching Hoofbeats,* Billy Graham, who has probably preached to more people in person than anyone in history, has written:

> I often join in worship with a small local congregation ....Because of its informality it reminds me of the early church. They gathered in small groups to sing, pray, preach, or listen to the Word. I enjoy a formal liturgical service, so Ruth and I sometimes worship in an Episcopalian or Lutheran service. On other occasions we enjoy an Assembly of God, Christian and Missionary Alliance, or Nazarene service. Actually God has given me a love for the whole body of Christ. I enjoy whatever type of service I attend.

The body of Christ is made up of individuals who may be different because of age, geography, travel, reading, employment, education, family, friends, heart, and mind. Yet, in diversity there can be unity—when the common focus is that of "looking unto Jesus, the author and finisher of our faith" (Heb. 12:2).

Needless division comes when we suppose that only the way *we* do things is right. Could it be that God has people he loves, people who know him, who do not attend *our* church? Can't one be our brother in Christ, even though he is not an *identical twin?*

As balanced Christians, we can have:

Differences without being difficult.

Diversity without division.

Opinions without being opinionated.

Disagreement without being disagreeable.

People who fail to understand these things, often go around with such a big chip on their shoulder, they are always out of balance!

To discern whether a church or Christian ministry is valid, we might ask: "What is their main emphasis—is it a man, a denomination, a divisive doctrine, or is it Jesus Christ?" After all, HE is the way, the truth, and the life— no one can come to the Father except through Him (John 14:6). There can be no true Christianity without Christ.

Because of Him, in the words of a great old hymn by Fanny Crosby (1820 - 1915), we can joyfully sing:

Blessed assurance! Jesus is mine,
  Oh what a foretaste of glory divine!
Heir of salvation, purchase of God,
  Born of his Spirit, washed in his blood!

Finally, the things we have presented in this book may be likened to a wide variety of foods in a cafeteria line. The food has been carefully and prayerfully prepared. As you have passed through the line, hopefully you have received some good spiritual food. If something did not ring true to you, you may take the meat and throw away the bones, if that is the case.

As I have sought to illustrate extremes that should be avoided, it has not been my intention to make light of people or magnify their mistakes. It would be better to make a mistake, trying to serve God, than to never try!

A balanced Christian does not have an "I'm-right-you-are-wrong" attitude, but always endeavors to "speak the truth in *love*" (Eph. 4:15).

A balanced Christian seeks to understand the *total* testimony of Scripture, without misapplying verses to prove a doctrine.

A balanced Christian avoids extremes, always seeking the *center* of God's will.

A balanced Christian is able to discern between that which is *essential,* and that which is *non-essential,* so that he does not major on minors.

A balanced Christian discerns extremes!